Meaningful
Minimalism

Meaningful
Minimalism

Align Your Life from the Inside Out

Dara Zycherman

Meaningful Minimalism

Align Your Life from the Inside Out

By Dara Zycherman

1. SEL027000 2. SEL031000 3. HOM019000

Library of Congress Control Number: 2025912744

Print ISBN: 979-8-9988007-0-2

Ebook ISBN: 979-8-9988007-1-9

Book design by Danielle H Acee, authorsassistant.com

Printed in the United States of America

ZK Publishing

Austin, TX

512-337-9219

DEDICATION

To Ann Zabaldo, my client, friend, and inspiration, whose maximalism has battled my minimalism with joy and humor every step of the way.

TABLE OF CONTENTS

How to Start

Picture this

You wake up. You get out of bed in your peaceful bedroom. No clothes on the floor, dresser, or bedroom chair. You pick out an outfit for the day with ease. You walk out to the kitchen, where a few dishes are in the sink, but it doesn't overwhelm you. Your kitchen is mostly organized and relatively clean otherwise. You don't let the little things bother you.

You check today's task list and calendar while you make your favorite morning beverage, adding a few extra items you forgot to jot down last night. But last night's planning ensured there were no surprises, which helps since you woke up a little later than expected. You find everything you need, including your keys and wallet, before heading off for the day.

You live your day with ups and downs, but you have clarity and confidence about the purpose of your day and are grateful for the (mostly) calm and aligned respite to return home to. Your home has the tools you need to live your best life. Most of the time, you know where to put things, and you don't spend much time buying things.

What's holding you back from living this vision?

For one, stuff.

The stuff problem

Picking up this book indicates that you have a stuff problem. Or that you think you are a disorganized person. Or someone bought it for you, and you're wondering what they are trying to hint at.

While you may know you have a stuff problem, on the day-to-day, your stuff exists as background noise. You may not hear it distinctly. Your stuff may be the wallpaper of your life, a visual, weighty annoyance, not prominent enough to force action. It's not a priority alongside other commitments, responsibilities, and of-the-moment interests.

Your stuff isn't only physical either. It's all the elements of your life: a committee you're on, a book club, a streaming service subscription, and that to-do list item to call an old friend.

This book will help you solve your stuff problem. Though maybe not in the way you expect.

This is not about organizing

Organizing is putting something in a recognizable, consistent place that it can return to and for that placement to make sense in the flow of your life. Organizing is a finishing touch, not the meaningful work or the complete solution to your challenges, stressors, or frustrations. It's only a piece of the minimalism puzzle.

My client Jake, a single forty-year-old man, lived in a one-bedroom condo. His place was large enough to hold all the stuff he owned. He could get to most of what he needed most of the time, if he remembered that he had it. He held multiple decades of stuff in his closet. Yes, it made navigating difficult. Yes, it was an eyesore. But it was day-to-day ignorable, save for losing track of mail occasionally. But as a social guy, his place was far from guest-ready.

His home was peppered with artifacts of his most recent ex-girl-friend. He lacked personal finance systems and a way to manage his aforementioned mail. His bathroom was filled with almost empty bottles that he kept to finish, even though he'd already opened a new one. He could get by, but his confidence, capacity to move on, and ability to host at his place were compromised. Jake's issue wasn't solely a lack of organization. It was also a lack of excavation and prioritization and a need to let a lot of stuff go emotionally and physically. Organizing was only a piece of his minimalism puzzle.

While the material stuff needs to be trimmed, home and lifestyle systems are difficult to create (if created at all). Emotions come out. People don't feel agency in their lives to make substantive changes that are true to themselves. I left Jake with a lightness and confidence that can't be shown in a before-and-after picture. His home was organized when we completed our work together, but more importantly, his life was elevated.

3

It all starts with family

One of my first "clients" was my dad. Growing up, he had a little setup in a room in our basement, which consisted of his childhood desk for paperwork and another desk with our family computer. The room became engorged as additional furniture, boxes, and un-sifted papers crept in. I give my dad ample credit for the four-drawer, tall filing cabinet filled with labeled and organized file folders and papers. He had the roots of organization, but there was always stuff poking out and around and needing assessment. He still felt stressed even though he never missed a bill payment. It was getting by in the best possible sense.

A few years after I started my adult life, he claimed my bedroom as his new office. I couldn't have been more delighted. He purchased new office furniture for the first time in his life. This represented a fresh start—it's never too late!

We brought up his old files and computer equipment to sort through and organize. I had fun finding old check registers from 1978 and his old Bar Mitzvah speech. But I couldn't help but ask him from time to time upon unusual finds, "Why did you keep this?" or, "Why is all this stuff randomly stuffed in an unlabeled bag?"

He had two go-to responses: One was the generalized "I'm not an organized person" excuse. (Not true! Remember the file cabinet?) The other was about how busy he was raising three kids. (This was true, though I know that a bit more organization and discipline could have saved him more time, not the other way around.) At no point did he acknowledge that we'd all been out of the house for years and he still hadn't found the time. We all tell

4

ourselves stories. That was his. You have yours. This book is mine.

When I would come over for subsequent visits and try to open the office closet door, he'd assume a look of panic and yell, "Don't open it!" I did anyway, and we continued to work through his stuff. I gave him systems to manage his sentimental stuff, let go of what he didn't need, and prepare him to handle incoming items. To this day, he uses the systems we put in place. I'm a proud daughter.

My dad is an excellent example of someone who paid the bills on time and has a successful life but whose life could have been improved and his stress eased if he had adopted a minimalist lifestyle. Being able to get by often serves as a reason for not taking steps to move toward minimalism. However, he and many of my clients suffer from a lack of ease and lack of control. They often feel overwhelmed and take longer to complete simple tasks. Five minutes here, ten minutes there, and a lack of confidence in these areas may not lead to financial collapse, but they will distract you from enjoying life's simple pleasures and taking on more meaningful tasks. Minimalism gives space for things to go wrong. It builds inner confidence in areas where you feel like an imposter in your own life.

You have your own parental stories that shaped how you organize, treat your stuff, and handle everyday sorts of adult responsibilities. Our ways of dealing with stuff often stem from our childhoods. Sometimes, we apply what we've learned. Sometimes, we rebel. If you're me, you make a career out of it.

Your personal history must be interrogated to understand and move past it.

My journey to Meaningful Minimalism

I grew up as a middle child in the middle of suburbia, living a middle-class lifestyle. I noticed that things that seemed untrue or lacked meaning felt uncomfortable to me. The man-made lake with fake swans in our neighborhood was emblematic of this, and I've been reaching toward a meaningful and aligned life since.

I also didn't like wasting time. I wanted all my time to be mine to do what I wanted to do, so I always found the most efficient path to complete tasks to unshackle my time. I wanted freedom.

I was taught the importance of family and spending quality time with people, the value of a dollar, and the importance of being responsible. These values resonated with me and have held true. Watching my dad work so hard to provide for us and seeing my parents always worried about money led me to think: If my parents are responsible, good people and live just below their means, I want to live far below my means so I won't be stressed as an adult.

While I'm hyperaware of stuff and wastefulness, I learned that most people are easily overwhelmed by it, ignore it, or don't know how to navigate it—much like how I have an awful sense of direction while many people have no need for GPS. Given my penchant for organizing and creating systems at a young age, I found myself being the organizer for friends and family. My initial experiences gave me insight into what people found most challenging, and I began to figure out how to help them best.

I read Duane Elgin's *Voluntary Simplicity*, which spoke of many of the same concepts currently packaged as minimalism and that

I had grappled with as an environmental science major in college. Elgin encouraged us to forge a "more direct, unpretentious, and unencumbered relationship with all aspects of our lives: the things that we consume, the work that we do, our relationships with others, our connections with nature and the cosmos, and more."[1] He viewed simplicity as honesty with ourselves, others, and how we interact with the world. If we live simply externally, we will be more inwardly rich. Reading his book early on helped create the premise for my minimalism ideology and likely shaped the early underpinnings of my Less Equals More business. It reinforced that my way of life wasn't crazy, even as I felt beleaguered at times, pushing against the status quo.

I learned more about sustainability while working at the U.S. Green Building Council, an environment-focused nonprofit. I refined my productivity skills, managed various projects with various people, and created educational materials. The concept of Less Equals More was born during this time as I tested the waters of professional organizing on the side. After a dozen years working there, I decided to leave to start my business.

Since I'd seen how organizing can make things look nice but cover up unplumbed issues, I wanted my business to embody the Meaningful Minimalism method I developed for myself. I wanted to *really* help people. I wanted to be the change I wish to see in the world.

Since then, I've sat with countless clients in tearful moments of letting go, triumphant disposal of painful memories, and

---

1 Duane Elgin, *Voluntary Simplicity: Toward a Way of Life That Is Outwardly Simple, Inwardly Rich* (HarperCollins, 1993), p. 25.

easeful smiles in newly simplified homes. I've watched confidence be rebuilt. The work got deeper than I had expected. (I will warn you, we will go deep in this book.) From new moms to retired divorcees to young professionals, I've witnessed throughlines in the human experience and the variety in between. We all can do better and be better.

The Dao of Meaningful Minimalism

While there is no universally accepted definition of minimalism as a lifestyle, there are common principles. It's doing the most with the least; only having what you need and most want, eschewing the rest. But our wants and needs aren't always easily delineated, and how does one do the most with the least? Simplicity is complex to create and beautiful to experience.

My method focuses on efficiency for the purpose of finding more freedom. In that regard, it's systems- and habits-based, and it applies to all areas of life: time, money, people, bath and beauty routines, email, activities, diet, and clothes. It's one solution that can be applied to everything, helping you integrate all aspects of your life and goals.

How I define Meaningful Minimalism:

Mindfully choose what you genuinely want and need. No more, no less. It stems from deep honesty within yourself and the pursuit of what is most meaningful to you. Minimalism is simplicity in all aspects of your life; seamless efficiency.

To clarify, the following are some minimalism *is* and *is-nots*, according to my approach:

Meaningful Minimalism is:

A framework and mindset. A framework is a structured way to think about a complex idea. It's how you think about your stuff and your lifestyle. The lens through which you analyze your life and how to change it. A set of questions and perspectives to problem-solve your life.

A lifestyle. We can't downsize our physical items without addressing how they integrate with what we *do*. This framework really is applied to everything.

A process and practice. It takes time to develop a new vision for your life, apply it, and iterate until it feels best and then continue to adapt as you change and grow.

A mindful and intentional approach. It's hard to be honest if you can't see through your own bullshit. Through mindfulness, awareness, and intention you can get to the root of your issues so you can take thoughtful actions.

A commitment to honesty. If you're not honest about who you are and what you stand for, your decisions regarding what to keep in your life and what to keep out will be misaligned with your reality.

An expression of agency. You can't blame anyone else for your lifestyle or piles of stuff. Likewise, you get to take matters into your own hands and challenge the status quo. You are in control, even when that means deciding how you want to react to the things you can't control.

An expression of self-compassion. When we are kind to and understanding of ourselves, we develop healthy homes, engage in mindfulness, and develop a positive self-image. The corollary is when we treat our homes like trash, let things land on our floors that we might trip over, or hold onto unprocessed emotions via our stuff, we aren't being self-compassionate or kind to ourselves.

Meaningful Minimalism is not:

An endpoint. You can't arrive at minimalism because your needs constantly change, and your belongings and lifestyle must adapt accordingly. You'll get closer to equilibrium and adjust more quickly to changes, but lifestyles aren't endpoints.

A design scheme. Minimalism was initially coined to describe a style of mid-twentieth-century visual arts and music. Often, people see minimalist design and minimalism as a lifestyle as the same thing. A minimalist home can also have a minimalist design aesthetic, but the aesthetic is not a requirement.

A one-size-fits-all dogma. What is important to you and your personality traits are what will populate the Meaningful Minimalism template I provide. A need for you might be superfluous for someone else and vice versa. There are few hard and fast rules.

Decluttering. Though minimalism will likely have that result, it'll do far more helpful things. The word *decluttering* masks the problem. The reasons for various areas of clutter accumulation may be different and require investigation(s). Sometimes, it's okay for things to be crowded or a little messy. You may need many colorful and meaningful objects on your desk for inspiration or as reminders. That doesn't mean your desk is cluttered if each is intentional and purposeful.

Social media design porn. Any room or closet can be made to look beautiful. A bunch of random stuff you don't need in a before photo can be half stuffed in a cabinet and organized (in a manner that is unhelpful) into pretty containers. You get a dopamine rush but learn nothing. It is easy to transform the look of a space. It is difficult but far more rewarding to do the work behind the scenes to downsize and simplify.

A trend. People have been living simply since forever. It's more challenging now to stave off the seeming abundance of things, opportunities, and potential tasks. The timeliness of this work and its importance continue to expand as our environmental problems exacerbate and our stress levels rise.

Consumeristic. That may seem evident at first, but if you have Meaningful Minimalism confused with the aesthetic of minimalism, or with organizing shows like *Get Organized with The Home Edit*, you may *think* you have to buy specific things to be a minimalist. You'll likely benefit by buying a few new things while transforming your life, but those purchases will be more intentional and functional.

Austere or heartless. Your minimalism adventure will be full of heart because you'll customize it based on your needs and what's most important to you. Regardless of how much you let go of, you'll be left with the stuff that supports your goals and priorities. The remaining space will highlight what's meaningful to you, which is anything but austere.

The application of Meaningful Minimalism is built on the foundation of mindset change. Your mindset is your mental attitude that governs how you interpret and respond to all situations. When you think about your life through a minimalist mindset, you interpret and respond to your stuff and your lifestyle choices in a way that reinforces your values and is streamlined and simple. Minimalism cuts through the noise and cultural morays. This book will guide you in developing that minimalist mindset.

How to use this book

Meaningful Minimalism is a shorthand label. This book is longhand.

I'll be up front: I want to brainwash you. Not in a cult-like or manipulative way. In a way that helps you break through your mental blocks and social constructs and helps you create a minimalist mindset. Why? Because willpower won't get you there. Willpower is rarely the best approach because of the relentless energy it requires. It leaves too much up to your current mood or focus. Mindset change is the most effective approach.

I want to make all aspects of your life easier; a holistic transformation.

I will espouse some things in this book that may sound extreme. Sometimes, when we hear or read things that challenge our basic assumptions, we can't help but put up our defensive shields. My ask of you is, after that shield goes up, wait a few minutes. There is a point beyond the initial clenching you may experience. Give it that space.

Don't keep a tally of bags thrown away to indicate your progress. This is about finding meaning in your life. Meaning doesn't hold a strict calculus. Keeping track of numbers is like counting calories when trying to lose weight. That information has some insight or value but doesn't teach you how to create healthy habits or unearth the emotions behind unhealthy food choices.

What's inside

This book is broken into seven parts. First, I'll help you define the *why* behind the work you'll be doing. Without clear motivation, making the most aligned choices for yourself will be challenging. Then, we'll dismantle the elements of your identity holding you back. That's when we start to rebuild: first by using a beginner's mind to question assumptions and then by rebuilding your mindset. At this point, we tend to get scared as we anticipate change around the corner. So, I'll address your concerns and fears (and excuses). Finally, I outline the steps to implement minimalism (this is the getting rid of stuff part.) and how to maintain it via continuous care.

First, read the book straight through so you understand the flow of deconstruction to rebuild and let some of these new and challenging ideas wiggle their way through your existing mindset, where it will meet snags and tears and "a-ha's."

Then, reread the challenging parts so they sink in more. Talk about them with your friends, unassuming coworkers, and the person you sat next to at the coffee shop. Talk about it with your therapist and write about it in your journal.

Sit through the tricky parts. Let your mindset change. While you can and should begin interacting with your home, stuff, and to-do lists along the way, mindset change will be your greatest asset. Throwing a bunch of bags into the trash won't get you to meaningful minimalism. The right type of personal investigation and planning will (which I will lead you in).

Adopting minimalism without humor or awareness can become another status quo-driven, unintended decision or worse, an oppressive paradigm. The freedom minimalism offers will be replaced by a different cage. If it helps, work toward being *minimalish*. Integrate the most compelling minimalist principles to the degree that feels comfortable and in a manner suited to your most pressing desires and needs.

If you're the type to go all in and never take a new idea with a grain of salt, tread trepidatiously. My intention wasn't to produce an overengineered strategy for you to follow. I have a lot of advice, but I hope you don't follow all of it. I invite you to open your mind to new ideas and perspectives and the opportunity to throw many of your assumptions into the compost bin.

You are building your very own version of a minimalist lifestyle.

Disclaimers

The names have been changed to protect the disorganized—except for my family members, who have pointed out that it would be very easy to find them given such an uncommon last name as Zycherman.

For just about every point I make, there are exceptions. To avoid pointing these out each time, I'm noting that here. Don't look for times when you're the exception to throw out the point wholesale.

The less financial security you have, the less some recommendations will be applicable. While some aspects of minimalism (e.g., how to streamline life administration tasks) can help anyone, I'm not discouraging someone who's financially insecure from buying in bulk when they are most likely to use up what they purchase.

For my fellow neurodivergent readers, minimalism can be especially helpful for you! However, there may be some more specific tweaks that would be more supportive of the way you think and live. My ADHD clients tend to get the most out of minimalism but may require additional strategies to augment what is covered in this book. I encourage anyone with neurodiversity to seek out other resources to use in conjunction with minimalism strategies.

For those struggling with depression, anxiety, or other similar challenges, a minimalism practice often pairs well with therapeutic support. As you'll see, there's a lot of emotional unpacking and getting to the root of it all. Both methods of work benefit each other. To be clear, I am not a therapist or doctor, and I'm not here to diagnose or treat any conditions. I'm just a professional organizer obsessed with minimalism.

Part I
Define Your *Why*

If you're about ready to dump an armful of stuff in the trash, you may want to put it down. There is a fair amount of thoughtful analysis and planning that prelude selecting what items will leave your home, not to mention organizing what's left. This pre-work begins with defining your *why*. What motivates you to adopt a minimalist lifestyle in the first place?

Your *whys* will be integral throughout the process. They personalize your version of minimalism and will frame much of your decision-making. But before we look at examples of *whys* that will ground your minimalist lifestyle, let's consider the backbone of why minimalism is worth investing the time to implement.

Investments that produce a *cha-ching!* of interest or dividends accrued in your bank account are not the only type worth making. When practicing Meaningful Minimalism, achieving your *whys* (and subsequently, your goals) is the return on investment (ROI) for the time and effort you'll be putting in.

Investments such as savings accounts produce minimal returns but have the least risk. Playing the stock market can lead to bigger wins but carries considerable risk. Minimalism is a low-risk, high-reward investment. If you let go of something you realize you need later, it's a minor impact compared to what you've gained in lifestyle improvements, especially over the long term. The high reward is freedom, time saved, more money (that you can invest!), calmness, and focus. You can't beat that deal. While there's no such thing as a sure thing when it comes to investments, minimalism is pretty darn close.

While we may recognize how, generally, our lives will become easier and more aligned with who we want to be if we apply a minimalist framework, it's the investment of time and energy to *create* a minimalist lifestyle that discourages many from undertaking this work. This is where you have to take a step back to see the bigger picture.

If we invest that time now, we don't get stuck later. *Later* is often an inconvenient time to address our stuff problems, with aching bones, piles too high to sort through, and complications of dealing with outdated technology or damaged items. Just as you miss out on more significant returns each year you wait to invest in your retirement account, the same is true with minimalism.

That's the long-term investment approach and benefit. The short-term payout comes with the saved time looking for that book of stamps or researching the best weighted blanket. Say goodbye to wasted time reviewing items over and over, never quite deciding to let them go, and to the latent distraction they create in the back of your mind. That static creates stress.

Meaningful Minimalism is only one-size-fits-all in that it's an approach accessible and applicable to everyone. But the *why* behind it and the exact outcome differ for each individual. As such, it's of paramount importance to define your own *why* and your personal motivators. So we'll first look at how to define your *why* and then some typical *whys* that you can adopt (or adapt).

Why Your *Why* Matters

There are three primary reasons you must get clear on your *why*:

1. It will keep you from giving up when things get sticky.
2. It will steer you toward decisions that align with your desires, goals, and values.
3. It will keep you honest.

If you're not clear on your *why*, you may succumb to giving away your decision autonomy to other influences and end up building your new lifestyle on an uneven foundation. We can't deconstruct our lives to rebuild effectively unless we know why we're doing it in the first place. So ... why are you doing this?

Consider the different categories of your interests and what's most important in your life in the material, personal development, ethical, social, and environmental realms. Go wide and narrow. Be open to surprises. Your *why* might be black-and-white and highly targeted, like wanting to start over after a bad breakup. Or you might pick up bushels of *whys*, some big, some small. In this case, be sure to prioritize them so you know what to do if they come into conflict. As we delve into minimalism through the lens of meaning, we have to acknowledge that meaning can be found in all these places.

At the end of Part 1, develop a draft list. Your *whys* will be tested as you read through the rest of the book and when you start downsizing. What you may have thought were your *whys* may not be present now, even if they once were.

A big *why* distractor: *shoulds*

My red alert beacon activates whenever I hear *shoulds* and *supposed tos*. These words and the sentiment behind them rule people's lives in a subversive way. They distract us from cutting to the truth of why we want what we want. *Shoulds* are a thinking construct you need to set aside in order to find your true *why*.

Shoulds come in the form of comparisons to others, withering old dreams, aspirational identities, and things your parents told you. They're the language prefix of cultural and societal norms. In fact, you're likely here, in part, because you think you *should* be. After all, a successful and meaningful life does not consist of ignored trash in your car, CDs from your punk phase, Leaning Tower of Pisa-style piles, and unreturned online orders punctuating your space. Being disorganized is frowned upon. So aside from your personal desires, there is the unnamed pressure of *should*.

These *shoulds* aren't limited to physical objects you "should" or "shouldn't" possess. How many times have you said that you *should* go somewhere: a dinner party, an out-of-town wedding, a happy hour, a family reunion, or the gym? It's typically said with reluctance and drawn-out syllables. Guilt or self-importance may be a driver. Or decision-making paralysis may lead you to go with the default *should* instead of the option you actually need or want.

Instead, ask yourself and answer with honesty: Do you want to go? What are the pros and cons? How does this stack up against the other priorities in your life? Is this about you or someone else? Is it about what you want someone else to think about you, whether or not it's true? For example, why would a friend or acquaintance want you at a party where you are going to be miserable or cause you to lose valuable time needed for other priorities?

I don't mean to imply that you'll have your optimal life if you only do things you enjoy. Sometimes we *choose* to do things we otherwise wouldn't want to, because of a particular situational context in which we see a meaningful gain. Think of all the times you helped a sick friend or family member. The actual activity involved probably wasn't exactly enjoyable, but the result was meaningful because you really did want to take care of them—not just because it was something you felt you "should" do.

Shoulds shouldn't matter. All these external pressures and disappointments in yourself for falling short aren't meaningless, but they aren't particularly meaningful either. *Shoulds* are clues, and you are now playing the role of detective. Keep a running list of these *shoulds* that come up, and consider how they play into your minimalism-related decisions. They will lose their strength over the course of this process.

Now that you're on the lookout for *shoulds*, we're going to look at some common *whys*. I hope these inspire you to identify your own *why*, but if they don't resonate with you, don't feel limited. It's worth the honest reflection of all your *whys*, as they'll guide you throughout this process and lead to your personalized minimalist lifestyle.

I Want My Lifestyle to Align with My Values and Goals

Every *why* we explore in the following chapters will address your values, your goals, and what's most meaningful to you. Who are we, after all, if not a product of what we believe in and what we're trying to achieve? Yet few of us experience full alignment between these intangible elements and our actual lifestyles. If you feel you're missing this alignment—or that you could better align your lifestyle with your values, goals, and meaning—this is one of your *whys*. For example, if having various types of freedom is a value, that should be part of why you are enacting minimalism in your life. Or, if you're not sure what your values and goals look like, the process of defining them can also be used as a thought exercise that may help you uncover your *whys*.

To further identify and investigate your motivation for minimalism, look at the building blocks of your life:

- What are you passionate about?
- What makes you cry?
- What do you want to achieve?
- How do you interact with family?
- What aspects of your past weigh you down?
- What are your secret dreams?
- What challenges you the most?
- Do you feel happy?

These big questions will provide fodder for defining your goals, values, and meaning.

The intersection of minimalism and goals

One of the first questions I ask clients is, "What are your goals?" I'm not asking about their minimalism goals but about what they want their improved life to be like and what they want to achieve. Then, when we're making downsizing decisions, we look at how our decisions can support their goals and ensure they aren't in conflict. As guideposts, goals keep us focused on what's most important. Having clarity on what they are makes it easier to create new systems and implement organizing strategies.

Defining our goals can be difficult, but we need them to successfully implement Meaningful Minimalism. The good news is, we can use the focus and simplicity that the minimalism framework offers us to help define our goals.

You may have a goal to be a world-renowned whittler. A minimalist lifestyle will help you accomplish this by allowing you to focus your discretionary spending on whittling tools, spend your time watching tutorials, and "carve" out space in your home for your craft's paraphernalia, organized in the manner best suited to your whittling whims. If your greater goal is to turn whittling from a hobby to a side hustle, being clear on that when embarking on your minimalist practice will not just affect whittling-related objectives but will also clarify your greater vision for home and other lifestyle choices.

Your goals may be in the vein of creating financial security or improving your health. Whatever they are, they will almost definitely change over time. They're not locked in, which actually eases the pressure a bit. With a minimalist lifestyle in place, you'll more easily be able to recognize when you need to make changes, and you'll have the tools to make them.

Your values and North Star

What are your principles? What's important in life? What makes you a good person? Your values closely relate to your ethical code and likely overlap with your spiritual beliefs, and they tend to guide your behaviors and decision-making. Your North Star is the beacon when life gets hazy and you are seeking direction. It's a fixed vision that coalesces your aspirations (i.e., your goals) with your values. It is your purpose in life.

Living our values makes life easier, as tempting as it can be to slip away from the more challenging ones. Otherwise, your life comes into conflict with itself. That's draining and confusing. I've repeatedly seen clients become stuck because their values, stuff, and lifestyle don't match. This makes it impossible to make strategic and lasting choices, whether they're deciding how to spend their time or choosing what purchases to make.

Some *whys* are rooted in values. Living sustainably and caring for the natural environment are value-driven *whys*, for instance. If you prioritize protecting the environment, you probably won't live alone in a four-thousand-square-foot home, drive a large SUV, or buy lots of single-use disposable products. That's not to say we're aiming for perfect alignment, just a conscious attempt.

Finding your North Star weaves together your sense of meaning and values with your ideal life direction in a shining pulse that leads you toward clarity. It allows you to set goals that align with your values, and it gives you a map with which to navigate anything life throws at you. When situations are emotional, or you're making big life decisions, your life becomes significantly easier when you can map back to your ultimate direction. And this all trickles down to the more minor decisions you make in your home and lifestyle.

What's meaningful to you?

Focusing on what's most meaningful to you is (obviously) the core tenet of Meaningful Minimalism, but first, I encourage you to question the common belief that meaning is intrinsic. We are in control of infusing our lives, and the stuff we clench, with meaning.

Sometimes we do this in a way that is distracting and causes further harm, anywhere from getting passed up for a promotion that was supposed to make our career's work meaningful, to infusing objects we own with meaning such that we hold onto them through guilt and sadness. But that meaning isn't central to the object or situation. *You* get to decide what things mean, and you get to choose what's most meaningful to you.

Articulating this meaning may seem daunting or a bit confusing if you've never thought about it before. Maybe you have a loose idea of what's meaningful to you but haven't related it to minimalism before now or haven't thought of meaningfulness as an important decider of what you own, how you treat those items, and/or how you manage your time and tasks.

For some, the list of what feels most meaningful is overwhelmingly long. Things are too meaningful. Focusing too heavily on our interests, passions, and sentiments can leave us overburdened and guilt-ridden when we'd rather spend a day eating cookies, watching silly movies, or working at a job that doesn't feel meaningful but isn't too stressful and provides the steady income to help us pay for other pursuits.

That's why it's not uncommon for our actions to diverge from our values—we are all hypocritical at times. But the more our values align with our lifestyles, the more confident and content we will be. There will be less friction, shame, chaos, and confusion.

Minimalism provides us with the clarity to identify what's most meaningful to us so we can start building our goals—and our entire lives—around what really matters. Implementing the minimalist framework intrinsically allows us to live our core values, guiding us to greater overall alignment.

If your *why* is to ensure your life is aligned, be sure to spend thoughtful time on identifying your goals, values, and North Star. Then, the next time you're shopping and deciding whether to make a purchase or consider letting go of something at home, you have clarity on what direction to take.

Before you go any further in exploring your *whys*, take some time to reflect on the values, goals, and sense of meaning that make up your North Star.

I Want Freedom

Feeling trapped in our lives is a draining daily struggle that leaves us feeling like we don't have agency. Your *why* might be to break out—your *why* might be freedom. Within this general pursuit, freedom comes in different forms. The common ones I see when applying minimalism are: financial, time, location, and freedom from influence.

Financial freedom

As we touched on, minimalism is an excellent investment. A simple life involves streamlining your personal finances so you never pay a late fee or miss a mischarge. You buy less and have less underutilized fixed payments like subscriptions. It involves constructing a financial strategy that is efficient and effective, leaving you with more money to invest, meaning a more significant future gain (i.e., "It takes money to make money."). Aside from proper budgeting and investing, living a simple and more minimalist lifestyle is one of the easiest and most rewarding ways to increase your financial security.

Minimalism is just about recession-proof. This doesn't mean that you won't experience *any* financial hardship. If you lose your job or have high medical expenses unexpectedly, that will be difficult regardless. But if you're living below your means and not stuck in a *Keeping Up with the Joneses* mentality (or *Keeping Up With the Kardashians* for that matter), you'll navigate changing circumstances more easily and you'll be able to effortlessly deal with minor fluctuations.

Oversized, overstuffed homes with multiple cars in the driveway and constant food deliveries can be a form of financial prison. The image may be enticing at first, but the backdrop of constant spending becomes a constraint (read: not freedom). Even maintaining our homes and possessions can be costly. Anyone who has cracked the screen on their smartphone or taken their car in for repairs knows the harsh truth of it, though they may forget in between these unexpected events. While financial freedom may be based on the amount of money you have, how it's used and your relationship with it are the determining factors for whether it becomes an unexpected prison.

With minimalism, we can save more money, either to invest or, if we are so inclined, spend on non-material goods that we also don't become dependent on. It would be great to spend extra income on a personal trainer or dance lessons. But if we ever need to make a change or are forced into a change, we could give these things up—that's freedom.

From wanting to overcome financial anxiety to longing for an early retirement, this freedom may have multiple motivators. So the *why* of this *why* becomes notable too. Is financial freedom a *why* because it provides you with the financial security to pay off all debts or generally makes you feel less anxious? Financial freedom also untethers us from unsatisfying relationships, neighborhoods, and potentially even careers. So, it's not just about the money.

Time freedom

Time is today's currency. We can afford to buy any number of gadgets, gain access to thousands of shows with one keyboard stroke, and grab the latest technology we didn't know we needed. But time is the one thing that has remained constant throughout history: twenty-four hours a day, seven days a week.

We want more time ... but for what? For time freedom to be a part of your *why*, clarify why you want it. Is it so that you have more peace and less stress (see the next section for more on this)? Is it simply to know that you have time flexibility? Is it because you have interests that require time that you currently feel you lack?

Time freedom connects to financial freedom along the lines of the old adage: "Time is money." Or the words of author Randy Komisar, who put it best, "The most dangerous risk of all: The risk of spending your life not doing what you want on the bet you can buy yourself the freedom to do it later."

Location freedom

Not being tied to a mortgage and the responsibility of homeownership allows you a different sort of freedom. If you choose to rent and have minimal possessions, you can move with greater ease. Maybe take a year off to travel or work remotely from an island. Minimalism alongside a flexible job can place location freedom in your grasp. Taken further, you can plan to retire early or take a mid-career, mini-retirement.

While nomadic roaming might not be your goal, having the ability to pick up and move without it feeling like an impossible or imposing task is an asset in our unpredictable lives. It's hard to manage a mortgage and home maintenance if there is a significant change in life circumstance. These may include a job opportunity elsewhere, wanting to be near a loved one, unforeseen medical expenses, or needing a different "vibe" at a new time in your life.

Even if location freedom isn't your *why*, it's worth keeping in mind as a potential benefit and something you may have access to if you significantly downsize. If you find that you could then live in a smaller home, it would likely open the door to living in a more desirable location.

Freedom from influence

I know it's hard to admit, but we struggle to think for ourselves at times. Especially when we're surrounded by influences that don't share our values, or we think an innocent social media scroll couldn't possibly steer us in an unintended direction. We think we're thinking for ourselves, but if you've created a lifestyle built on *shoulds*, your *why* may be to break from our consumerism-based society. That doesn't mean you won't still have the freedom to buy something you really (really) want, but at least you'll know it won't be because you were unduly influenced by marketing or societal pressures. Minimalism will shake things up.

You can make a point to listen to different points of view and not live in an echo chamber. Having full, realized agency means that we are discerning in our interpretation of all influences. Freedom from influence means we can take in information and analyze how it matches our values so we make wise decisions for ourselves. This skill will carry you through the remainder of this book, whether or not it's a *why*. But if this is something you've struggled to find, it will sit as a powerful freedom of the spirit that extends beyond downsizing.

Yes, I see the irony of me spending the entirety of this book trying to influence you while encouraging you not to be influenced. But by choosing to read this book, you are exercising your desire to make a change in your life and considering whether what I say resonates with you.

As with many of the things we most want in life, there's an opposing force. We desire more freedom while we also fear it. Our burdens become blankets. We identify with our lack of agency. Much like the fear of success, the fear of freedom seems so counterintuitive that we don't recognize when it's holding us back. Watch out for it.

Freedom's benefits are hard to quantify but are terribly enticing. Is freedom one of your *whys*?

I Want Calm and Relief from Overwhelm

Most of my clients come to me because they feel stressed out. Whether it stems from the frustration of tripping on some things while losing other things or missed bill payments, they recognize that making big changes in their home can give them relief. Aside from the practical and immediate results of minimalism, their strongest motivator is to create a calm home and be less overwhelmed. And with a minimalist lifestyle's holistic approach, the resulting peace will extend beyond the walls of their home. Their *why* is an emotional state.

Living in a chaotic environment can affect your mental

health. You're not crazy—it's neuroscience. Since our brains prefer single-tasking (versus multi-tasking) and order, the unfettered distractions in your home create a competition for focus. This is the source of your mental overload. While you might be someone who can ignore these distractions to some extent (which may be your disorganization challenge in the first place), many experience this stress.[2] Minimalism is about streamlining our attention to what's most important, reducing the anxiety caused by too much stuff.

There are other related stressors. How about the overwhelm of people coming over, prompting you to have to hide your stuff in any nook and cranny you can find? Followed by the stress that comes when you can't find these hidden items. Negative self-talk and guilt over not being more organized ignite more pressure. You may even carry the worry of how your disorganization may be taking a toll on some of your relationships.

While a disorganized home itself causes overwhelm, it's also overwhelming to think about starting to organize. After you've started, there will likely be more stressful moments. This is a temporary state to notice and manage, but avoid letting that prevent you from making this investment. Highlighting how important this *why* is to you will help you persist through.

Warning: Calm can feel eerie if it's a foreign emotional state.

---

2 Erika Penney, "Why is a messy house such an anxiety trigger for me and what can I do about it?" The Conversation, September 3, 2023, https://theconversation. com/why-is-a-messy-house-such-an-anxiety-trigger-for-me-and-what-can-i-do-about-it-211684.

You may even be attached to your familiar chaotic state—change has its challenges, even when it's the change we're seeking.

No matter how much fun we want to experience outside our homes or the welcomed liveliness of guests inside our homes, we want our abodes to be some sort of sanctuary. Or at the very least, we don't want them to be the cause of the very stress we want to escape. If you felt tension releasing just from imagining what it'd be like if you had an organized and streamlined home and calendar, a pursuit of calm might be your *why*.

I Want to Be Resilient

Personal resiliency is a less common reason people build a minimalist lifestyle. But I encourage you to consider it. We build our lives too thinly, where one wrong move or unanticipated event can send us spiraling. Overbooked schedules are like the moment before the last block in Jenga is removed. Overstuffed closets and cabinets are no different. We approach life believing that we control so much more than we do right before it unravels. We have another option, however. We can acknowledge the complex realities of life and build intentionally around them.

Resiliency is the skill of recovering quickly from adverse situations. Unexpected life events and significant life transitions can't knock you down. You can withstand a recession or pandemic. You are adaptable when you live more lightly and are strategic about where you put your attention. You are clear on what you want and need and are accustomed to not consuming for consumption's sake. It's like preventative health strategies to eat well, exercise, and visit a healthcare provider before a problem worsens or develops in the first place. You reduce the chances for problems proactively and are well set up to combat problems if they arise. Of course, minimalism doesn't erase the problems or result in nil emotional impact. But it keeps things less complicated and more transparent.

When you begin to evaluate what you genuinely want and need in your life instead of thinking, for example, *What can I afford for rent and what budget should I set to get all the things I want each month?*, you might ask yourself different sorts of questions like, "Should I spend less than the rent I can afford? Would I still be able to get a place I like while allowing myself additional financial reserves? Even though I can rent a larger place, will I have the time or physical wherewithal to clean the added square footage?" Since resiliency includes your financial systems and practices, this ties in with minimalism's ROI and the financial freedom it can help provide. Being resilient involves asking the right questions and having the strength to make tough decisions.

Developing resiliency of mind and heart is an intricate effort. It comes with experience, time, and a certain inward tenderness. Practicing mindfulness can help. With mindfulness's perspective on non-attachment and witnessing our true selves, most of our things won't feel like a loss if we have to say goodbye due to a life transition or economic hardship. Our emotional balance and connection to ourselves is a stalwart resource. If this is your *why*, understand that while you'll be implementing minimalist strategies outwardly to build resiliency, this is a long game and involves more inner work.

On a personal note, I'm divorced. And no, getting rid of a husband wasn't an act of minimalism—though the clarity that minimalism affords leads to directed decision-making and room to focus on the most pressing issues with less distraction. I never felt the urge to remain in the relationship for the creature comforts or to maintain the advantages of home ownership and shared resources. Though my life from the inside out was shaken up, the pragmatic effort of untangling our lives and dealing with the "stuff" of it all was surprisingly simple given our minimalist life infrastructure. I had the confidence to deal with all that comes with divorce despite the emotional weight of the transition. I credit my development of resiliency and minimalism as the source of my fortitude.

Resiliency, like maintenance, is an unsexy aspect of life. Yet, doing it well leaves room for more of the fun stuff we want, along with added easefulness, even during more challenging times. You make room for the sexy stuff. Things that aren't costly to maintain or constantly need replacing are more resilient than the opposite. When tragedy strikes uncomplicated lives, the disaster can be mitigated with more focus and less fallout. By sustaining our lives effectively, we can maximize joy and fulfillment. An effectively maintained life contributes to minimalism and resiliency, and vice versa.

Minimalism today leaves us with less loss tomorrow. If a significant life event hits us hard, we have more wherewithal to charge through. Resiliency is an asset that pays off, almost like buying an insurance policy. Only you create it, hold it, and can pay it out to yourself as needed. That's why minimalism is best implemented before you're swimming in disorganization or find yourself in a financial tight spot. You make the most thoughtful and appropriate lifestyle decisions when not in crisis. If you want to become more resilient, then this is one of your minimalism *whys*.

I Care About the Environment

Minimalism is a pathway to living sustainably, whether this is a *why* for you or not. From consuming less to being intentional about the material content of products, minimalism and sustainability go hand-in-hand. However, identifying sustainability as your *why* will help you highlight areas where environmentally friendly practices can be integrated into your minimalist lifestyle, in addition to being a meaningful motivator as you plow through the downsizing process.

If you're on the fence about whether this is a *why*, it may be illuminating to examine what we mean by sustainability and the natural environment. We often consider environmental issues and the natural environment on two different planes. We mentally disentangle them to enjoy the beach while not considering rising sea levels due to climate change. That would be a real downer while catching a tan.

Everyone has a relationship with the natural environment. Everyone's story and connection are unique. Perhaps you've fished your whole life, are a cross-country skier, or feel uncomfortable camping because you've always been a city dweller. Maybe you love buying flowers from the farmer's market, or you grow vegetables in your garden. If you're wondering whether nature is your *why*, start by dissecting your relationship to it. And if it is important to you, you can expand that to include environmental issues. To help you get started, we'll look closer at some of the issues plaguing our planet, how they relate to the products we consume, and how minimalism can help us navigate these issues.

Sustainability challenges abound: the Amazon burning, endangered species going extinct, climate change, resource scarcity, all forms of pollution, water insecurity, loss of biodiversity, ocean acidification, rising sea levels, urban sprawl, nuclear waste, natural resource depletion, and littering. This is only a short list. Earth is our home, and it has never been more troubled. We can't assume an unknown person or entity or *science* will come in to rescue the planet.

The issues are complex, and that complexity can become a barrier. Occasionally, we interact with these troubling realities directly in our daily lives (e.g., breathing polluted air or throwing something in the garbage). Other problems seem to happen "over there" and not affect us (e.g., melting polar ice caps and deforestation). It's difficult for most of us to understand the myriads of Earth's systems and how they interconnect.

We have trouble connecting our in-the-moment activities with their consequences because of cognitive dissonance (when a person's behaviors and beliefs don't match). The bigger, far-reaching, and complex the consequences, the more links in the chain, which makes us feel more disconnected. This is why, despite all the evidence of humans' negative impact on the environment and how most of it will come back to bite us, we continue making environmental problems worse.

Environmental issues affect more than frogs and ferns. They also negatively affect those in poverty, living in undeveloped countries, and lacking political power. While hurricanes can destroy multimillion-dollar homes, the least wealthy and empowered suffer the most. However, we all experience the negative effects of these issues, and unless big changes occur, they will only worsen.

So, given this complexity and peril, what can you do? First, you can educate yourself more about sustainability issues without putting pressure on yourself to know everything. Then, you can decide whether to be mindful of specific environmental issues (or all of them) when implementing your minimalist lifestyle. It's a decision to think beyond your personal challenges and accept that your actions alone will not "save the planet." In other words, do "the right thing" regardless of the result, if it's important to you.

One sustainability issue closely related to minimalism is material resource use and waste. With the exception of humans, nature does not waste. Bears dig into trash cans; they don't throw anything in them. The natural environment and all its organisms have evolved to eat, shelter themselves, exercise, and play without waste. Nature is inherently efficient.

Waste has many unintended consequences—many of which you can't see or likely don't imagine. Landfills not only take up space and are unsightly, but hauling trash to them also involves energy use (and usually carbon dioxide emissions, which contribute to global climate change). Landfills release leachate (a contaminated liquid), polluting our aquifers and waterways. The creation of single-use, disposable products also creates the unnecessary use of natural materials, energy, and water.

Also, some seemingly green strategies aren't as effective as you think. For example, recycling is touted as an environmentally proactive action. Instead of the landfill, an item has a chance for a second life. It's the better choice between the two but only marginally so. After plastic has been recycled once, it cannot be recycled again. If there aren't buyers for recycled materials, they go to the landfill. Often in the collection and transport of recycling, a fraction of these materials become litter because of wind and carelessness.

Buying a so-called green product is similar to recycling. If you're purchasing a new product anyway, it's better to choose the more sustainably sourced version. But buying a green product is still buying a product. Often, products touted as environmentally friendly are only marginally so, if at all. So questioning if you need something new is the most environmentally conscious action.

For any new product, energy—likely from non-renewable sources—and water are used to extract, manufacture, and transport the natural resources from which it is made. We forget the buildings and warehouses used to house raw supplies, laborers, offices of those companies, product packaging, and final product placement in stores. As such, it's difficult to ascertain how sustainable a product is, so learning about the basics of sustainability can be helpful. However, it is nearly impossible to have a complete understanding of the environmental impact of a given product.

I'm not suggesting you stop recycling or buying green products wholesale, but rather to connect the dots on why having less stuff is better for both the environment and yourself. Minimalism decreases the number of times and ways to analyze the best material-use approach.

While the complexity of environmental issues need not be studied for this to be your *why*, it's helpful to learn a bit more, unpack whether you're experiencing cognitive dissonance, and decide whether you want to incrementally integrate more sustainable lifestyle choices. Also, keep in mind that as you apply minimalism to your lifestyle, you still have countless choices to be more or less eco-friendly when it comes to how you let go of items, how you use items, and which ones you acquire.

Each of your actions may be more or less sustainable than you realize. Minimalism clarifies and sweeps away so many possible decision points and trade-offs. By having less, you don't have to figure out which product is the most environmentally friendly because you're not acquiring the product in the first place. Life can be simpler *and* more sustainable. And while you don't have control collectively, neither does each drop in the ocean. But enough drops become a wave.

I Want My Lifestyle to Align with My Spiritual Beliefs

Most religions and spiritual practices align well with minimalism. They generally encourage us to be genuinely kind, focus on generosity rather than greed, and respect ourselves, others, and the Earth. Whatever your religious and spiritual inclinations, minimalism can help you align your life with those beliefs.

If you want to practice your spiritual beliefs through your lifestyle, instead of only at a meditation sitting or Sunday service, that desire may be one of your *whys*. Discern how your personal application of your religious faith or spiritual inclination aligns with minimalism. To get you started, we'll touch on some Eastern religions and philosophies, followed by the Abrahamic religions. (Please note that this is not meant to be a comprehensive guide to religion and minimalism, but a springboard for inspiration as to how you align your own religious beliefs with your Meaningful Minimalism practice.)

Eastern religions and philosophies

In Western culture, we frequently borrow postural positions, calmness, and silent moments from Yoga, Buddhism, and the practice of mindfulness without necessarily spending time understanding their significance. When you get under the hood, you may find that elements of your *why* exist within these disciplines.

For example, modern posture yoga (i.e., yoga classes at yoga studios and gyms) is just one component of Yoga philosophy. There are also moral and ethical guidelines for our behavior toward others (*Yamas*) and personal practices we conduct to treat ourselves with care (*Niyamas*). The other components are breathing, focus, and meditation.

Within the Yamas, many guidelines line up almost perfectly with minimalism. Take *astheya* (non-stealing), for example. This doesn't simply cover a mugging in the park. It considers stealing from the Earth, the future, and ourselves. We can even steal from others by comparing ourselves to them—feeling like we are lacking or superior in some way. This often happens when we see that others have things that we want—material-wise, friend-wise, you name it.

Some practices within the *Niyamas* also align with minimalism, such as *sauca* (purity and cleanliness). While the focus is on the body and using tools like breathwork and diet, this practice includes organizing and simplifying your home as an extension of yourself. It emphasizes the connection between a cluttered space and cluttered mind. Purification helps us distinguish what is true from all the other stuff that distracts us.

Buddhism's foundation is the Four Noble Truths: (1) suffering exists; (2) suffering arises from attachment to desires; (3) suffering ceases when attachment to desire ceases; and (4) freedom from suffering is possible by practicing the Eightfold Path (ethical and personal practices that lead toward nirvana). Essentially, Buddhism teaches that attachment, or expectation of something happening or being a certain way, is the root cause of distress. We wouldn't feel so bad if we stopped wanting things we can't have. This goes not just for material items but for life circumstances as well.

The feeling underpinning wanting to own something that we believe is beautiful instead of simply appreciating its beauty is a manifestation of the second Noble Truth. If we can't own that thing we desire, we feel down. That lousy feeling may come in the form of frustration that we don't have enough money to afford it or regret at a missed opportunity to purchase it. Then, we may be even more inclined to pursue the next thing we want so we don't suffer again.

We also develop emotional attachments to the items we already possess: our grandmother's old china, the broken watch that our grandfather handed down, the ninth-grade science project that still brings us pride, or even the carpentry project we began but never finished. These attachments are strong, and the effort to break free from them is daunting. So we hold onto these items. However, instead of addressing each of these items one at a time, we can simplify the process by applying the principles of Buddhism. We can practice non-attachment more broadly.

We seek out permanence, thinking everything is concrete, when in reality nothing is. For many, this is an unsettling thought. But with minimalism, we can begin to let go of the need to hold onto the things we own.

If the core principles of Yoga and Buddhism resonate with you, educate yourself to gain more than a surface-level understanding and application of its teachings. Then, see if this becomes one of your *whys*.

Judaism, Christianity, and Islam

You may have been raised under one of the Abrahamic religions and still practice or, if you don't actively practice, some of your perspectives likely still originate from its principles. Or you may be somewhere in between. Wherever you are on this spectrum, if one of these religions holds meaning for you, keep reading.

Stemming from the Old Testament and the premise of a singular god that created the world, the Abrahamic religions share some common insights while expanding in different directions and practices. With the premise of God creating the world, environmental consciousness can be viewed as a way of respecting God. And as we've discussed, sustainability goes hand in hand with minimalism.

All three religions teach us to be kind to others and to those in need, which would encourage prioritizing donations as a means of possession disposal. These values also encourage us not to keep things we don't use so others in need can have them. Some Islamic holidays even require giving to those in need as part of the ritual. Islam provides these paths to curb hoarding that may happen without thinking.

In addition to the Ten Commandments, these religions have various restrictions like keeping Kosher (Judaism) and Halal (Islam). While not directly related to materialism, these practices teach followers to restrict their consumption. An intentional effort must be taken to acquire foods to meet these dietary restrictions—and may make followers feel different from their peers as a result. Saying no to food others enjoy teaches that just because something can be consumed doesn't mean we're entitled to it. Eschewing foods that don't meet these dietary restrictions promotes the sort of self-discipline that minimalism requires.

In Christianity, Jesus spoke directly about materialism. His teachings encourage investing in your spiritual practice over your possessions to make your afterlife glorious. In other words, store up your treasures in heaven instead of seeking comforts on earth and caring what people think of you. Riches are an impediment to a spiritual life because, as we gain wealth, it's common to put faith in the material world rather than God. Judaism also encourages *mitzvot* (good deeds) over materialism as a way to focus on internal spiritual pursuits rather than the external goals that materialism fuels. Whether you believe in God or not, the question of how much faith to put into the material world versus less tangible things is part of this *why*.

Similarly, Islam dissuades showing off or being ostentatious. This is a way to be thoughtful to others and eschew materialism.

While enjoying your life and experiencing the fruits of your labor is encouraged, Islam directs you toward doing this reasonably and respectfully so as not to provoke a feeling of "less than" in others. In a sense, this helps others not covet, which is one of the Ten Commandments. Coveting is closely tied to minimalism as a fair amount of consumption is instigated by seeing what others have and thinking, *I should get to have that too!*

This is not an exhaustive description of the connections between these religions and the components of minimalism, and there may be other important religions and spiritual philosophies in your life that you can use as your *why*. Consider looking deeply into your belief system and analyzing how it's applied to your current lifestyle and where there's misalignment.

Finalize Your *Whys*

Be sure to consider other *whys* I didn't list, like those related to building self-esteem and self-confidence, or creating a lifestyle that will prepare you for a potential partner. Perhaps improving your physical health is a *why.* This would steer you toward kitchen supply and organization, grocery shopping, and exercise decisions. It would even help you prioritize cleaning out dust, mold, and bug and rodent "leftovers." Disorganized homes are often dirty (or obscure dirty areas), and implementing minimalism can help you lower the risk of asthma and other associated negative health outcomes.

Once you have your *whys*, allow them to deepen and unfold throughout this iterative process of minimalism. We will revisit these in Part 6: Put It into Practice as you develop a vision for your new and improved life. We start with your *whys* and end with your *hows*.

As important as it is to define newly articulated *whys*, take a moment to reflect on your old ones. What are the deeper reasons you're in this mess? What are the old *whys* that you'll be replacing with your new minimalism-supporting *whys*? Unpacking old beliefs requires us to question our upbringing, social connections, and cultural dispositions.

This is why most people nip around the edges instead. The time for nipping is over! Release your *shoulds*, clarify your *whys*, and see that this path toward minimalism has little to do with stuff and more to do with why you have your stuff and obligations in the first place.

An aligned and meaningful life awaits.

Part II

Let Go of Your Identity

Who are you?

Now that you've clarified your *whys*, it's time to loosen the grip of *who* you think you are. Your identity includes many attributes. But here, we're focused on the parts of your identity that relate to how you acquire, display, and maintain your stuff and day-to-day lifestyle. Your home and everything in it may represent the person you used to be, think you should be, wish to be, or want others to see. We allow our stuff to meld with our identity or use stuff as a placeholder to define ourselves when we struggle to do so otherwise.

During the minimalism process, we often hold ourselves back by assuming our identity is fixed. This prevents us from making changes that would allow us to live more authentically. Untangling stuff and identity will ensure that your stuff supports you rather than weighing you down. Along with your *why*, you'll get closer to alignment with what matters most to you and how you want to develop your simpler life. The minimalism process itself will be easier and more efficient.

How do we begin to detach our stuff from our identity? As with most challenges, we must first recognize the problem. Acknowledging how closely our identities are wound up with our stuff will allow for a new perspective as we look around our homes. Then, we need to unpack and rethink our identities. This analysis makes letting go of stuff easier and more in tune with who we truly are. We'll examine how identity holds us back from developing a minimalist lifestyle and do so without trying to "be" a minimalist.

Identity Types

You may think of yourself as a collector of artwork. Or a gamer. Or a musician. Or a crafter. Or someone who is always prepared. To be these identities, we must have the stuff that supports the associated activities. When we move away from these activities and interests, we don't want to lose our identity, so we keep the stuff. When activities or interests become your identity, releasing the associated stuff may call into question your identity, creating resistance to moving on.

We accumulate stuff aspirationally but don't use it, either because we've changed since acquiring the stuff or it's just not enough of a priority. We obtain or keep things to appear a certain way around others, perhaps seeking external validation; for example, having a bookshelf of "interesting" books (whether or not we liked or read them) and collectibles from our travels so that guests think we're smart and well-traveled. It's not for us; it's for them.

Even the curation of products, knowledge, and expertise can be considered an identity. For example, my client Scott, who was the go-to person in his community for fix-it tasks, found sharing his knowledge and having materials to share to be enriching. However, he took it to the extreme, allowing his self-appointed role to become disruptive to his home life. Storing all of his supplies was a hassle for him to manage, and it also bothered his family because some of these materials took over common spaces in the house. Additionally, buying a storage unit became necessary, adding an expense to the family budget. So while he was helping others, this identity prevented him from letting go of some highly specific items and sizes of common items because his identity was so wound up in being the go-to person for this type of help.

Here's another identity to shed: I'm a disorganized person. If you attach yourself to this identity, how will you ever make these crucial changes in your life? It doesn't mean you're helplessly disorganized if you've failed to downsize and organize well. It probably means you tried in a way that didn't suit your needs. Or you weren't fully committed to or emotionally ready to begin the process. Organizing may not be your strong suit, but you likely organize some things well. Defining yourself as a disorganized person is a dismissive identity that will hold you back.

These are only a handful of examples, meant to unlock your thinking and consider what identities you hold.

We Change,
but Our Stuff Doesn't

The overabundance of stuff in our homes is a symptom of not addressing or recognizing our personal evolutions. It's not only that we have too much stuff for our current needs, but we also still have items that were meant to support past needs. Maybe they did the job well once but no longer do. It's time to move on. This messes with our notion of our identity. And why we need to go through this practice of letting it go.

When we change personally, and our stuff doesn't change along with us, it becomes wallpaper. It's so familiar and constant that we can't see it because we see it all the time. It is ignored unintentionally. Unlike computer operating systems that tell us immediately and constantly that they need to be upgraded, we have no such reminders in life. As a result, we hold on to these possessions, systems, and entire homes longer than is necessary.

At the opposite end, there's the stuff that we've convinced ourselves is still helpful because we think we haven't changed (even though we have) or believe it will be useful once we re-engage with a past activity or aspect of our lives. Think about craft projects, cooking supplies, or exercise equipment that we tried only once or maybe even used regularly a long time ago. We've mildly convinced ourselves that we will engage with them again someday. But we've changed, and that someday is not likely to come. And if it does, in ten years, is it worth keeping these items along for the ride? Or finding space for, maintaining, and moving them?

Sometimes, we feel good recalling our past through representative objects. Sometimes, emotional attachment begins with this happy feeling or sometimes with a sad or even painful one. But often, keeping items we are attached to is the default rather than an intentional exception here and there. We may have an old uniform or tee shirt attached to the good memories, but the memories won't escape us, even without the item. Sometimes, we choose to keep the things we failed at and remind us of tough times. They may be the most difficult to address when we change. Tracking our failures can be a real drag and not allow us to fully embrace our new life.

You may need to let go of your aspirational identity as you change. This may be the toughest of all identities to release. To be clear, I'm not suggesting you delete your active aspirations. Keep and nurture those. But be careful not to wrap yourself too closely with an aspiration far from being fulfilled and not prioritized. Maybe you used to make beautiful pottery but gave up on it while still considering yourself a ceramicist. So every time you used one of your mugs or someone asked to see your latest creation, you felt terrible disappointment in yourself. You never became the ceramist you aspired to be. This aspirational identity hurts. Instead, you can aspire to do pottery again as a hobby or one day pursue this art full-time, but since it's not your identity, your current self is not in constant conflict with that idea of who you are.

We also change as a product of our environment: city to the suburbs, adapting to new technologies and roommates, apartment to house, cold to hot climate. While more external in nature, these changes can lead to unnecessary stuff in our homes because we bring the stuff that represents our old needs—even, say, something as basic as a pair of winter boots—to our new home in Miami. While less deep and emotionally driven, these changes must be addressed in the minimalism process.

It is overwhelming to consider sorting through our past lives and current aspirations. It is heart-wrenching to say goodbye to the person you used to be, as the piles continue toward toppling. This excavation is also time-consuming, so gathering and holding on becomes the default. Many struggle with change because it feels uncomfortable, and we seek the things that make us feel most stable and safe. You must recognize that you've changed, reopening the discussion of identity with yourself to eliminate the stuff that no longer serves you.

Our stuff should never hinder us, tie us down, or be meaningless to our current lives. That's why we have to tackle the disconnect between our current selves and the stuff we hold onto, whether it's our past self or our aspirational self.

We Let Others Create Our Identities

Most of my clients are trapped by the identities given to them, and our work together seeks to break them out of these invisible straitjackets.

It starts in childhood and never lets up. We're subtly trained to give up our power to make autonomous choices by letting others tell us our identities, and then we start to believe them. You may have excelled in English and social studies and were thus considered "not a math and science person" (or vice versa). This may have limited your interest in growing in the opposing direction.

Most of us desire to be understood and valued. So when

people put their perception of who we are on us, we might feel bad correcting them or assume that they know us better than they do. Sometimes, we put more weight into who people think we are instead of looking more deeply into ourselves and pushing back on these misunderstandings.

Aside from people's perceptions of our supposed identity, there are also general expectations of who people want us to be. This can creep into our identity as well. On a grand scale, it might be imposed upon you to be married with children, own a home, or have a particular career. This can deter you from creating your own identity that is true to you. It may be why your *whys* are unclear, not just as they pertain to minimalism but also to your life as a whole.

It requires us to look at our lifestyle choices with discernment. As you look through the stuff in your home, do you see an untouched piano that you've held onto because your parents drilled it into you that well-rounded individuals must know how to play an instrument? Because the minimalism process asks you to look closely at your stuff, why you have it, and whether you might want to let it go, you have to face this question of identity. And in doing so, you regain the agency you lost when more passively accepting someone else's identity imposition.

You don't have to explain yourself and any of the future changes you'll make as you grow. Don't give your power away to someone else. Be honest about who you are, even to the people around you who (often innocently) try to tell you otherwise.

Our Stuff Makes Us
Self-Centered

As we discussed, we can attach our identities to our things and look to our things to define us. We assume people will be just as excited and interested in our stuff as we are. There is a self-centeredness entrenched in our stuff: all our things and memorabilia, our trinkets and old blankets, well-worn tee shirts, and museum-like childhood bedrooms. It's all about "me."

No one wants to be considered self-centered. Yet we do this with our homes daily. Everything in our home feels important. And the stories behind them? Even more important. Accumulating stuff when it doesn't relate directly to our most basic human needs is extra. And all that extra comes with a set of stories we tell ourselves about why we need the item, even though we haven't used it in years or didn't hear about its existence until yesterday. We believe these things make us interesting people. Our things say: I am here!

Self-centeredness comes in the form of being so preoccupied with our stuff. That preoccupation involves researching, buying, maintaining, rearranging, thinking about whether to keep what, contemplating the intertwined emotions, and resisting letting go. We can donate items, give them a new home, or dispose of them most sustainably, but this is often sidestepped in favor of keeping these items because they have even the most minor significance. We renege on our desire to give to those in need or take a more sustainable approach because we overvalue or misunderstand our needs. So it feels too difficult to part with certain possessions.

Acknowledging the self-centeredness of it all can be tricky. We all take ourselves too seriously sometimes. When we come face to face with this reality, we can begin to untether ourselves, seeing materialism for what it is and laugh at how seriously we took it.

We're not bad for keeping some heirlooms, kitchen gadgets, or hobby paraphernalia. But we should not see them as holding a special importance because we can say, "This is mine." Treating our stuff with a degree of reverence can be a slippery slope in the direction of self-importance.

Introspection of this sort can be quite uncomfortable. Sitting with it, sans self-judgment or guilt, is key in veering your life toward simplicity. There are many methods for this sort of mindfulness: a full array of meditation techniques, journaling, therapy or counseling, somatic movement, or art. Use this perspective as an antidote to the stories of your possessions' value and why you need the storage unit or extra bedroom.

Undoing this self-interest is surprisingly easy once you pass the intellectual hurdle because stuff can never be you. And conversely, you will never experience true fulfillment from stuff. You can enjoy it with appreciation but then be ready to let it go. Removing the self-centered nature of stuff helps us untangle our identity from it.

Busy-Person Syndrome

Busyness is the disease of our times. It corrupts your mindset and isn't necessary for your survival or basic needs. However, you can discipline yourself to recognize when you rely on this trap for comfort or artificial meaning in your life.

I'm busy is blurted out by people with a fair amount of choice in their daily lives. While I'm not dismissing a demanding job, raising children, or unforeseen circumstances as disruptive, time-consuming efforts, I want to question your mindset on busyness. Thinking of your life as an endless to-do list, thankless, or a series of appointments is missing the point.

(Unintentional) self-centeredness is often a component of the busyness plague. Busyness may reflect an ingrained cultural sense of self-importance or an attempt to make oneself feel important. Extending this in the other direction, it's also a way to reassure oneself that life has purpose. If you aren't on your smartphone while cooking dinner and running late to the next "thing," what is your worth?

Those with the most chaotic or frenzied lives are often trying to avoid loneliness or avoid acknowledging that they feel uncomfortable with themselves or lack meaning and passion in their lives. It's hard to feel lonely or confront difficult realities when things are constantly being asked of you, and you always feel behind. Your busyness may be a placeholder for true meaning.

When you address the balance between the abundance of opportunities and the things you need to do, you can begin undoing the construct of being busy. For example, a friend and I shared a list of activities we wanted to experience together. At one point, I looked at the list and said, "We've barely done anything!" I felt we'd squandered some of our time together with less exciting activities instead of planning time for these listed pursuits. She reacted oppositely, saying, "But that would be so sad if we had everything crossed off the list. Then there'd be nothing to look forward to. There's so much fun stuff for us to do!"

I've come to believe, begrudgingly, that she was mostly right. She highlighted the abundance of interests and opportunities for adventure together. This was a beautiful thing I was missing in my desire to be productive and plan well. I was taking seriously what was supposed to be fun. A balance is needed: Make the effort to do things that matter to you but enjoy that you're lucky enough to have so many opportunities for joy and depth.

Similarly, consider your life as full or at different levels of fullness. When your life is made up mainly of the things that have meaning, it doesn't matter how "busy" you are. Instead, you can feel satiated. If life becomes too full, or you are drowning in so much nonsense that it erodes the relaxing or recuperating time you need for balance, it's time to make a change. This will allow you to operate as a full, content person, not a busy one. The aim is not perfection. The aim is your North Star, adjusting as you go along and not taking what you have for granted.

Simple word choice substitution and mindset change can move us away from "busy" and toward "full" as part of the transformation we're developing. *Busy* feels like a complaint. *Full* acknowledges that a lot is going on but it has more agency behind it.

If at any point while reading this book, you defend yourself or make an excuse for inaction because you are "too busy," I'm not buying it, nor should you. This word covers up what's going on, much like passing off any type of disorganization or volume of stuff as clutter. It's just as insidious as labels are: too general to have any true meaning. Avoid passing off the responsibility of your current life construct to the headless busyness monster. If you look under the bed (i.e., deeper into yourself), you will be confronted with the fact that this monster does not exist.

Destroy Your Identity

The first step in letting go of these identities is to parse out which ones are true for you and which are not. For those that are not, you can select what objects or lifestyle choices are no longer needed. For your true identities, you loosen their grip when deciding what to include or not include in the more minimalist life you're creating. Like the example of Scott, it may align with your values to help others, but finding balance and drawing appropriate boundaries are essential.

The outcome of unpacking your identities isn't about becoming a particular type of person. At the core, it's the opposite. It's about becoming more you. Loosening the stranglehold of identities you've created for yourself or others have created for you is a rite of passage in developing a minimalist lifestyle.

But don't trade the identities that no longer suit you for a new one: A minimalist. You've come to the wrong place if that's your intention. I've read stories about people hoping to hop on the "trend" of minimalism. They got rid of the stuff they thought they were supposed to. They had the "right" number of shirts and shoes and spoons. And then they realized they weren't happy. They wanted to become minimalists instead of designing authentic, intentional lives.

Being a minimalist is not who you are; it's a framework for thinking about your life and implementing coherent strategies. Become minimalist-minded, not closed-minded.

Part III

Question Everything

We've started to question everything by unpacking our *shoulds* to get to our *whys* and then release or loosen our identities. Along the way, you probably began to question some things: long-held assumptions, the choices you accepted rather than made, and why you still have a yearbook from middle school. We need that strong *why* established to brave through questioning, well, everything. And relinquishing our identities leaves us more open to new possibilities that identities can prevent us from seeing.

Were you feeling uncomfortable before? Buckle in. We're going to break down your assumed reality here. The good news is that questioning many underpinnings of life can be enlivening.

Minimalism is a question. Like most other questions about our lives, this one asks us to be honest. It asks us first to clear our minds. Then, it asks us to perform inner work and coalesce that work with the external practicalities of life. To balance personal histories and emotions and pragmatism.

Like all questions, how and when you ask influences the answer. If you ask these questions when you're already frustrated, the answers will be rash. If you ask them when you're at a store filled with goodies that capture your desires, you may lie to yourself. If you frame a question such that keeping an item in your home is the default and backed by fear, you'll end up owning more than you need.

Even when we know the questions to ask, they can lead to less question-asking due to overthinking, overanalyzing, and decision fatigue. We tend to over-question ourselves when there are diminishing returns for us and under-question ourselves regarding our lifestyles and the stuff we accumulate. Also, information overload tends to make it more challenging to make decisions. Knowing more can be counterproductive.

The tail end of questioning everything is looking at potential unintended consequences. We need to question everything because some of what we do, buy, and think might be aimed at a particular goal but, in practice, does not achieve its intention. Unintended consequences often can't be predicted, but we can look out for them and learn from them.

This section tackles the under-questioning part. We'll explore several ideas you probably haven't spent much time questioning—and you really should.

What's the (Real) Problem?

What's your problem?

I don't mean that confrontationally. I mean it sincerely. I rarely tell people that they have a problem. I only help people who believe they have a problem work through it. People come to me with various minimalism-related *challenges* but haven't properly or fully defined their big problems. Their challenges are closely related but aren't necessarily the same thing.

As we've discussed, this is not about becoming a minimalist or another such identity or being disorganized in some fashion. Identifying the real problem is crucial because, if you don't, you will either cover up the symptoms of that problem or you won't be as efficient and targeted with your solutions. Using a minimalist mindset, we want to save time and effort. So being as clear about the problem as possible will maximize our ability to solve it well, with the least effort.

When you look around your home or office, do you experience the following thoughts and feelings: overwhelm, chaos, hopelessness, uncertainty of where to begin, lack of time to address issues, frustration, embarrassment, fear of judgment, shame, disappointment, disgust, at a loss, along with the thought of *If only ...*? These reactions are strong and sometimes defeatist. But they aren't the problem statements that will allow you to identify your real problems. Though they are meaningful inputs.

First, consider the internal problems. These are the nonphysical things about you and your lifestyle that are problematic, from which the feelings perpetrated by looking at your mess stemmed. These may be casualties of personality traits and life choices you either embrace or desire to improve. For example, you may feel busier than you really are because you don't manage your time and schedule well. The problem here is actually a time management problem, possibly coupled with a prioritization problem. For both, one would have to dig deeper to determine their flavor. Is the prioritization problem due to wanting to "do it all" and not actively prioritizing, or is it hanging on to old priorities or *should* priorities that no longer apply? You can dig deeper into these as well!

Next, consider the external problems. These can be related to your possessions or day-to-day processes. These are physical possessions in your home, your car, and anything else you own that cause you stress, aren't organized, or that result from a shopping problem.

Also, your home itself. Maybe you chose to live in a larger space than necessary because you thought it would display your success or that you "needed" the space? Process-related external problems may include: bill payments, time spent trying to find an overdue library book, email management, meal planning, relationship demands, and getting dressed. These activities relate to living a simple life even though you typically don't "see" them when looking at your home.

Review your brainstorm lists. They're likely similar to what you thought your problems were but perhaps offer a deeper level of insight and a couple of surprises. Remember: This exercise is a starting place. More insights will rise to the surface as you continue through the book.

If the list only reads, "I'm disorganized," dig deeper and try again. The problem may be that you are too tired to put things away at the end of the day. It may be that you have plenty of time to put things away; you just don't know where to put them. The problem may also be that you could organize, but you are so overwhelmed that you give up. Or it might be that organizing doesn't come naturally to you, so you need help setting up systems that work best for your lifestyle. Maybe as an adult, you're rebelling against your parents, who were strict, frugal, and oppressively organized.

If you're unsure how to drill down to the real problem, a possible approach is the Five Whys (not to be confused with the Define Your *Why* process in Part 1). The founder of Toyota, Sakichi Toyoda, devised this approach to uncover technical-problem causes. It breaks down larger or opaque problems into its individual components.

First, name your problem, then ask yourself, "Why?" and then ask why about your answer … five times.

Problem: I rebuy items I already own.

1. Why? I can't find the item I already own.
2. Why? I don't like to spend much time looking for it.
3. Why? Because looking around feels unlikely to produce results.
4. Why? Because I have little idea where to look.
5. Why? Because I don't have a specific home where I keep each item I own.

There may be a lot to unpack here. It may be a Russian nesting doll of questions and answers. It's worth getting down to the smallest doll. That's where the root of the problem lives.

The worst way to solve a problem is not to define it correctly. With well-defined problems, we can devise more appropriate solutions.

Systems and Imagined Realities

To question everything, we must step back to look at the big picture. We must recognize that we're a part of various systems we didn't create, didn't necessarily choose to be a part of, and don't always know we're in.

A system is a set of connected things forming a more complex whole. But many systems are difficult to analyze and tricky to unravel or undo, and they may change at any time. They may pile upon each other or intersect. Some systems we see; some we don't. Some of these systems work well, and some don't. Correcting or abandoning problematic or inefficient systems can be incredibly difficult because of how easily we are wedded to the ideas within them, and because no one person owns them.

These systems may be an education system, the company that employs us, the current political system, or the transportation choices in our local area. Beauty standards are sort of a system, as is how credit plays a role in purchases and other financial pursuits.

Not knowing you are within a system and being unable to see outside of it can leave you with limited choices, restrained creativity, lack of perspective, hopelessness, and stuckness. These are all the symptoms, which end up feeding into your resistance to making big changes when downsizing. That's why questioning everything, including these systems, is paramount to simplifying your life.

We can start identifying systems, analyze their role in our lives, and then question the hell out of them.

These seemingly invisible systems are akin to the concept of "imagined realities" or "social constructs." These are shared stories among a population that are so ingrained, powerful, and widely accepted by the group that they're almost the same as reality. Reality is the soil outside your house and the body you inhabit. But most of what we consider reality has been thought up by humans.

This concept is expertly explained by Yuval Noah Harari in his book *Sapiens: A Brief History of Humankind*. Yuval writes, "Unlike lying, an imagined reality is something that everyone believes in, and as long as the communal belief persists, the imagined reality exerts force in the world. ... As time went by, the imagined reality became ever more powerful, so that today the very survival of rivers, trees, and lions depends on the grace of imagined entities such as the United States and Google."[3] The power of imagined realities overcome us in such a way that we don't know we are partaking in them, and, in turn, they exert incredible control over us by default.

That means we typically have some sort of choice. And even when agreeing to partake in a system or imagined reality, it's the "agreeing to" that will serve you the most significantly. You will feel in better control of your choices, even when they don't feel much like choices. We humans need water, food, and shelter to survive, in addition to other human connections. But we technically don't have to wear clothing in temperate climates. Even though we don't have to, it's a cultural agreement most of us have made. It's a system we are agreeing to, much like money.

This is where minimalism comes in to encourage us to identify and investigate the systems and social constructs we are buying into and see which ones we want to opt out of or amend. You may be surprised at what you find: systems you didn't realize you were a part of, systems you can exit, systems that can be less prominent in your life, and systems you can interact differently with to make them work better for you.

A common system that comes up in conversations about minimalism is the "American Dream" of homeownership, complete with the idea that, in order to be successful, you have to own a

---

3 Yuval Noah Harari, *Sapiens: A Brief History of Humankind* (New York: Harper-Collins, 2015), p. 32.

large home with multiple rooms for different purposes. This system goes mostly unquestioned. It's viewed as a non-negotiable that a large home is needed from a financial perspective (it's not), to hold all of your stuff (much of which doesn't get used), and in order to host guests. My client Todd had bought into this system, and as we unraveled it for him, he was shocked to realize he didn't need to fill every shelf with things or every room with furniture. Within our homes, the ingrained ideas of the "American Dream" drive us like laws.

When we look at systems like beauty standards, technological "needs," and desirable transportation methods, the concept of "deserving" starts to creep in. The desire to fit inside the system may go deeper than what you think you *should* do—it may start to feel like a right you've earned. But in reality, no one *inherently* deserves anything, and thinking we *deserve* to fit into a certain system pulls us away from reality and, ultimately, boxes us right back into those *shoulds* we've worked so hard to dismantle in previous chapters. Understanding that you aren't beholden to any given system—for prestige or any other reason— takes the pressure off when deciding what you really want to keep, part with, and acquire. It becomes about basic needs and wants, regardless of the constraints of any social constructs or systems other than those you actively choose to inhabit.

As you start to look at the world through systems and imagined realities, it might feel unsteady. All of those "It's just the way things are" reactions may now have a different tone. But there is a freedom in seeing things more clearly; more of the decisions you make when implementing your minimalist lifestyle will truly be yours. You will begin to regain more of your agency.

By recognizing imagined realities as what they are and seeing them starkly against things that are truly real, you will be able to question things more easily. It doesn't mean that partaking in an imagined reality is intrinsically bad—some are great! I'm only positing that engaging in them blindly is a trap that makes change nearly impossible.

Just Say No to
the Status Quo

While systems and imagined realities must be brought to light, the work doesn't end there. It's important to use your *whys* and values and North Star to question them. But that's a broad approach. Let's boil things down to more recognizable and smaller-scale status quo situations that are a bit easier to peel.

To do this, I need to talk about Christy.

Christy was more organized than most of my clients. She brought me in at the end of her purging project to help with the more difficult stuff, from both a logistical and emotional standpoint. While wrapping up one day, she said that she was struck by something I'd said:

She didn't need to take the bag that the dentist handed to her every six months at the end of her appointment.

This was a revolutionary idea for someone in her sixties. Every time she received a travel-sized toothpaste tube, a toothbrush, and floss in that little plastic bag, she never thought to say no. Here's the thing: Most of us buy and use our own brands. We think we're going to take these freebies along on our travels, but we don't typically because we want to bring our own stuff or travel for longer bouts that don't require travel-sized items. Or if we want to use the freebies, the half-used-mini-tube is icky, lost its cap, or expired. We save them for guests, but guests almost always bring their own stuff. And the amount we save for travel or guests, even if needed in a pinch, far outweighs the number of items that we will use. We only need a set or two, if that, to be occasionally replaced (*maybe*).

We're coaxed by the "just say yes" mentality when someone gives us something, the excitement of free stuff, and stories we tell ourselves about how we're actually going to use or give these away in some fashion (often creating more work for ourselves in the form of, let's say, buying a container to store this stuff).

Upon a trip to my sister's, I stumbled upon an entire shoe-box-sized plastic container of toothbrushes. She always bought special toothbrushes for my nieces, and she and my brother-in-law used electric toothbrushes. While a few extra toothbrushes might have prevented a trip to the convenience store if a guest needed one or if one accidentally fell into a toilet, the increasing volume over a decade was ultimately unhelpful.

Staying on the theme of bath and beauty supplies, I spent thirty years washing my hair with shampoo and conditioner. First with products that contained chemicals and then the organic variety. All came in plastic bottles. All seemed as necessary as wearing clothes and brushing my teeth. It turns out that one's hair can look and feel just as lovely without these wasteful products.

Through a bit of experimenting, I stopped shampooing entirely. Instead, I rinse my hair with arrowroot powder and vinegar every few weeks. That's all it needs to stave off oily buildup. The vinegar adds a nice shine too. Since I have curly hair, oiliness is less of an issue than dryness, so conditioning is needed to ensure I don't look like I just stuck my finger in an electrical outlet. Through more research, I found chemical- and package-free conditioning bars to circumvent the need for plastic bottles. These have become more popular recently, but over a decade ago, questioning the status quo of shampooing and conditioning took intentional effort.

We've all been led to believe an unquestioned reality, and because these are all basic purchases or freebies, it's easy not to *think* to question them. But the status quo isn't always the best. Now, when designing your minimalist lifestyle, you can interrogate each assumed belief and its merit.

Is your bathroom really too small, requiring an extra set of plastic drawers, or is it that you've accepted the status quo to buy certain products and collect unneeded freebies instead of questioning it? The bathroom and its associated products are a microcosm of this status quo assumption.

We do this with other objects in our homes like bedroom furniture. Do you need a headboard, bed frame, or large night tables? Or consider other lifestyle habits like getting haircuts every six weeks or subscribing to all the streaming services. Any of these can be a part of your minimalist lifestyle, but did you first consider the system or status quo that led you to assume it's needed? Be sure it's because you think they're meaningful, and do so thoughtfully and intentionally—not because you think you're supposed to. This status quo questioning will make you feel more confident in the lifestyle and products you retain and more open to letting go of things you hadn't considered before this mindset shift.

The Hidden Costs of Stuff

We have to question how much our stuff is costing us, and to do that, we're going to dissect the hidden costs of stuff.

We assume the cost of something is its purchase price. It's partly why we feel great when we get something for free (even if we don't need it) or on sale (even if we wouldn't have bought it otherwise). Aside from the purchase price, there are invisible financial, time, and emotional costs. Until you understand what these are and associate them with items you bring into your home (purchased or otherwise), you won't be able to decide whether acquiring a particular item is worthwhile.

Let's break down these hidden costs.

Hidden financial costs

Sales

Buying an item on sale is its own sort of rush. It can make you feel like you gamed the system or got one over the big guy. It may make you feel rewarded for being a sales sleuth or full of luck to stumble upon such a deal. Either way, buying an item on sale makes us feel good.

However, sales can lead us to buy more than we need or to buy something we don't need at all and wouldn't buy otherwise. While we save money at the onset, the purchase might not be advantageous because of the other financial (and time and emotional) costs of stuff.

Interest

Putting aside mortgages and car payments (even though they suffer from this hidden costs issue), what items have you purchased using a payment plan in which interest must also be paid? Have you incorporated this extra cost into the "cost" of the item? When using a payment plan like Affirm or Klarna, you also need to follow all the rules, which, if you don't, could result in you having to pay more or pay at a time when you assumed you'd have more cash available. If you can't pay your credit card bill in full and owe interest, the products you purchased on that card technically cost you more as well.

Unobserved or uncategorized credit card transactions

Other hidden financial costs come in a different form: the inability to easily and accurately understand your spending. Monthly subscriptions are a common culprit here because the "monthly" aspect hides how much you spend on a product or service per year. While other products you buy are once-and-done, these can be never-ending.

How often have you glanced through your credit card statement to see a site like Amazon listed multiple times without knowing what categories of spending it included (as opposed to, say, a clear category like a restaurant)? Given the wide-ranging nature of items you purchase, not being able to see what those categories are leaves you with a skewed understanding of your spending. This may not address the hidden financial cost of a particular item but rather the hidden nature of what categories of items you spend on. You can't manage (or budget for) what you don't measure.

Storage units and moving
If you have so much stuff (including the stuff you inherited or accumulated for free) that you need a storage unit, those items have a hidden cost that should be assigned to the items stored. Additionally, you should consider the costs for bringing and moving the items to and from the storage unit (for example, paying for a truck, packing materials, or a full-service moving company). Also, when you move to a new home, you have associated moving costs regardless of how much you move, but as the volume increases, so do the associated moving fees.

Sets are a setup
In the movie *Father of the Bride*, a financially stressed Steve Martin wheels his cart through a grocery store. He makes quite the display

as he rips open hot dog bun packages, (humorously) enraged that the number of buns is greater than the number of hot dogs in a package. He views it as a conspiracy between the hot dog and bun companies meant to rip off the American public. He doesn't want to pay for four buns he doesn't need.

While sets may not be conspiracies, the point is clear: We buy things we don't need to get the things we do need.

So often, clients have sets of things and only use a portion of what's in the set. They believe their options are to keep or let go of the whole set. This is not the case! Break up your sets with abandon! Be free of your constraints! Only on occasion is a set best kept together for resale value, but this is rare, and you should do some research before assuming your grandfather's old train set is worth a small fortune.

A client of mine, Andy, purchased a new vacuum and received a cache of attachments. This overwhelmed him as he saw it as a homework assignment to watch a half-hour-long video that described the use case for each. (None of which was articulated in the vacuum's manual!) Instead, I suggested he pull out the few we determined were most relevant to his needs. Saving all of them together was not a requirement to resell the vacuum if it came to that. He sold the majority of attachments in the set, made a few bucks, and didn't have to decide where to store them.

Consider whether you buy sets even when you only need singles, your fear of breaking up sets you already have, and how you deal with the sentimentality around Granddad's train set and other heirloom sets. Avoid buying sets unless you need all the pieces, and don't keep elements of sets you don't need and that, therefore, come with all the hidden costs of having stuff.

Beware of bulk buying

It's tempting to buy in bulk when that means your purchase is cheaper per unit. Fifty rolls of toilet paper at 50 cents apiece versus ten at a dollar apiece seems like a no-brainer. But more often than not, saving money by buying in bulk leads to spending more in the long run.

How confident are you that you'll use the bonus third bottle of shampoo? You may not be thinking at the moment about how often you switch beauty products or how long it takes to get through those bottles. Many bathroom products eventually expire. You may have less available space than you'd prefer, leading you to buy more storage containers and spend time organizing and rotating products, potentially forgetting that you bought those extra things you already had because you had shoved them up on an unrelated shelf!

There's a financial trade-off worth considering. We focus financial savings on buying more than we need for a better price, even if we don't need the items or are at high risk of not finishing them. The wastefulness happens downstream, making it easier to ignore. This financial equation requires more mindful accounting.

Planned obsolescence

Planned obsolescence is another marketing scheme. It's when a product is planned or designed with an artificially useful life. In this way, it becomes obsolete either from a purely superficial standpoint or a functional one. By understanding planned obsolescence, we can see the economic attempt to encourage us to purchase multiple versions of a similar product in a short time span.

Let's consider some examples. After several years with my cordless vacuum cleaner, it only released small bursts of power. I called the company to find out what was wrong. Turns out, the battery was caput, and because it was an old model, they no longer sold replacement batteries. Five more iterations of the vacuum had been released since I purchased mine. I'm willing to believe its technology or features improved a bit, but the version I had suited my needs. It was a high-end vacuum cleaner, not a rocket ship. How much better could it get? Still, I had to purchase a new one and replace a product that should have lasted longer, and the many iterations in a short time span were clearly not huge jumps in technological advancements. This is planned obsolescence.

Need I mention the smartphone? Plans are offered so that phone owners receive the newest version each time it's released. Minor feature advancements are lauded, but most people only use a few basic features regularly. Replacing your phone before it breaks is rarely financially advantageous. Most problematically, it's not designed to last.

Aside from technology, the fashion industry is essentially planned obsolescence at its core, with trends being part and parcel of its appeal. It perpetrates this scheme in two ways: superficial and functional. Superficially, by creating trends, a beautiful and desired top becomes passé in a couple of years. Nothing has changed about the top other than the fashion culture around it. Regardless of whether you follow fashion, there's a low-level cultural response when someone is very clearly dressing out of style. It may unconsciously lead you to believe that the person has poor taste or lower financial status.

From the functionality standpoint, cheap clothes are produced only to be worn a season or two before they fall apart. Then consumers purchase more clothes in addition to determining what's worth fixing (since sometimes clothes are cheaper to rebuy than mend). Saving money by purchasing cheap clothes that quickly need to be replaced rarely saves you money.

The hidden cost involves buying into a system that will require more purchases. This doesn't mean that you should never buy a vacuum cleaner or smartphone, but it emphasizes the importance of thinking forward, investing in longer-lasting products, and not getting swept up in the idea you need something you don't. While you may occasionally and intentionally decide to purchase the new tech gadget or trendy top, be sure you include all these hidden costs and planned obsolescence marketing schemes in your calculations. (And if sustainability is one of your *whys*, consider the cost to the environment.)

Pricey maintenance
Laptop not working? That's going to cost you. While spending to maintain an item you already have is almost always the more eco-friendly choice (and only sometimes a big money-saver over buying a new item), it's important to know how pricey and likely

this maintenance will be. It's also helpful to consider whether you can do the maintenance yourself or will have to pay a service provider. It can be as simple as clothes that can only be dry-cleaned to as involved as the purchase of a car. Consider amortizing these extra costs, along with the purchase price, depending on the likely need for repair during the product's lifespan.

Emotional costs

The purchase
Financial decisions associated with making purchases are often emotional ones. Sometimes, those emotions stem from how you were raised, your current financial position, or your beliefs about your financial competency. Remember the financial stress your parents experienced outwardly or that they ignored while putting your family into debt? Maybe they never taught you how to manage your money or make you feel guilty about most purchases. Regardless, we have many entrenched beliefs and emotional sensitivities when it comes to our parents, and financial ones are no different.

We experience emotional responses to self-investigation about our responsibility (e.g., Can I afford this? Should I be saving instead?). Maybe you feel bad that you can't afford something or wonder whether you should save the money for something else or be responsible and put money in your savings account instead. Often, personal belief in our own financial competency is riddled with emotions and comes up right before (or immediately after) purchasing something.

Sometimes, we try to eliminate one emotional stress by creating a new problem. For example, if you're worried about whether you can afford something but really want it anyway, you might stress yourself out spending time researching every possible place you can acquire the item at the least cost. This may make you *feel* more competent even though you've spent significant emotional bandwidth (and time) to get something that you, perhaps, still can't really afford.

The process of making a decision to purchase an item and initially sitting with the choice may involve a range of emotions, including guilt, regret, self-criticism and letdown (if you don't receive the rush of instant gratification). And this is only the beginning of the emotional costs.

Post-purchase or post-acquisition

Whether you were the original buyer or received an item as a gift, you will often come to the point where additional emotional costs accumulate:

If, after immediate post-purchase, you realize you don't want something anymore, and it can be returned, but you can't locate the receipt or have any stress around the return.

If it's past the return window, and you realize you shouldn't have purchased it, you feel guilty (and may keep the item to assuage the guilt).

If down the line you realize you don't need something anymore, you use emotional bandwidth to wrestle with issues like: Why don't I have a bigger home to store this in? Who can I give it to who will love it as much as I did? Why won't anyone buy it for what I think it's worth? Why do I buy so many things I don't need???

If someone else gave you the item, you consistently consider it for removal but revisit guilt again and again.

These may not be high-intensity emotions. Some may just be borderline thoughts. But they all take something from you, especially considering all these micro-moments in accumulation.

Example of the emotional cost of a free item

My client Carla texted me with a problem. Her sister, who owns a house, has been storing a vintage chandelier for her for about a year "for free." Carla didn't have a place to store it or a house to install it in and didn't know when she'd be able to purchase a house. Since she acquired the chandelier for free, she could save money and have a chandelier she loved if she bought a house. She would then reacquire that fixture from her sister, who lived in a different state.

But her sister texted her, asking what to do with it because she was clearing out the storage area she was keeping it in. Carla asked me what to do: Store it at her parents' house instead? This would involve two more people in her quest to save a chandelier she really liked but didn't have a plan to use.

My advice was to have her sister get rid of it, along with all of the other stuff she was already letting go of, so it wouldn't be added effort for her and because it didn't make sense for her to keep this "free" chandelier. She didn't have room for it in her current apartment a few states away. Not to mention it might not work in the home she might eventually buy at an undetermined time.

"Even if there's free storage? Should I really let it go if it can save money in the future?" she asked me. She was stressed out, reaching out to me and having trouble making a decision, and it wasn't clear that this would save money in the future.

"It's not free. *If* is the operative word," I told her. "You don't know when you're buying a house and what you'll need or want at that time."

"I feel bad she's been storing it, and now I'm just saying *never mind*. This is why I need to stop involving other people and planning for 'what if I can use this one day,'" she told me. A lightbulb moment!

Time costs

Time costs range across the purchasing continuum:

The purchase

Initial research to decide what to acquire, shopping time, unboxing, untagging, sorting through packaging and pieces (e.g., what to keep, recycle, throw out), determining whether the product works or fits, setting it up, and understanding its component parts.

Post-purchase or post-acquisition

Whether you decide to keep an item or let it go, there are time costs involved here as well:

- Returning: The time it takes to submit the return online and then drop off for shipment. Or, sometimes, forgetting to return something in the required timeframe and then needing to figure out what to do with it. Or realizing it's too much of a hassle to return, keeping it, and then having to, again, figure out what to do with it.

- Selling: Deciding to sell the item online, taking pictures, writing up a description, posting on a few sites, fielding questions and coordinating pickup (and dealing with no-shows), or packing and shipping time if mailing the item.

- Keeping: You're happy with the item! Great! But that means you must maintain it by cleaning, fixing, moving it around your home, updating it, figuring out how to store it, and eventually reorganizing it.

These time costs are intertwined with emotional costs because of the emotional weight of having these conversations within ourselves and with others, along with the actions we spend time on due to the emotional costs.

They're intertwined with financial costs too, because time is money. I have a friend who could charge a lot per hour for his technology skills, yet he spends an inordinate amount of time researching the best flight prices. While he travels often, the cost savings of the research is often not worth the sheer amount of time involved.

Avoiding the costs

One more hidden cost: me. Professional organizers and minimalist coaches like myself are, in part, a hidden cost of stuff. This is also true of the cost for junk removal companies and cleaners (especially ones that do some organizing and tidying up). If you need to hire other people to help you in various ways with your stuff, that's another hidden cost that hits the financial, emotional, and time buckets.

Identifying the hidden costs doesn't mean you should over-analyze each purchase or never purchase something with substantial hidden costs. Instead, recognize where the hidden costs are more clearly to determine whether an item is worth it. Empower yourself with information and clarity to make decisions that align with your values and goals.

Tackling *What-ifs* and Rationalizations

"But what if I need this someday?" I hear this question from my clients on repeat.

We get stuck on *what-ifs*. These occur when we ask ourselves a litany of questions that result in keeping an item because there is *a chance,* regardless of probability or importance, that we may use it one day. These *what-ifs* are closely associated with all the rationalizations we concoct to acquire or hold on to stuff. Instead, question those *what-if* questions and all the rationalizations along with them.

Let's dig in: What is the likelihood of the *what-if* scenario coming true, and what would be the consequence of it not being true? *What-ifs* pose as pragmatism when sometimes they are low-grade fear. If you dig beyond your assumptions, your underlying fears emerge. Instead of framing the question as *What-if I need this someday*, ask yourself how bad the consequences would be to let it go. Try assuming you've let it go unless you can make a bulletproof case for keeping it, which will help prevent misunderstandings about what you should keep. Ultimately, you'll spend less effort on whether to keep something while making better choices.

The cousin of *what-ifs* is the rationalizations that solidify our decision to keep or purchase something and (mistakenly) make us feel good about it. Most of us are exceptional rationalizers. Often, we know what we want to have and then build up a case to defend why we should have it. We devalue the cons and focus on the pros. Defending our desires and actions is a skill we begin to sharpen at childhood. The better we get at it, the more we can get away with it, and the more confidence we can feel about our decisions. But not all reasons are created equal. To make more aligned choices, we have to sharpen our discernment (i.e., calling ourselves out on our own bullshit).

Some typical general rationalizations for things we already own include:

- "It's small and doesn't take up too much room."
- "My children may want this one day."
- "I made this."
- "I've just always had it."
- "It was expensive so I'd be wasting money if I let it go."
- "People always compliment me on it."

In addition to general realizations, we devise specific reasons to keep a particular item. These make their way into our minds as "facts," leading us to believe our decisions are rational and perhaps even responsible! It's challenging to undo this pattern.

For new products, we may conduct endless research to pick the best thing and hold triumphant the good deal we got. With our seemingly solid list of reasons for the purchase, we feel resolved. If we reopen the issue later (should I let this item go?), we find that this list remains nailed into our mindset. Pulling out nails is a pain. No matter how reasonable your reasons sound to yourself and others, they may not stand up well in the face of the bigger picture of creating a minimalist lifestyle. (We'll address this more in the Decision-Making as a Skill chapter in Part 4).

Rationalizations and *what-ifs* are questions of risk tolerance. Risk tolerance is difficult to define, if considered at all. Some minimalism-related risk tolerance questions range from *Am I willing to risk paying $10 for this item again in a few years if it turns out I need it?* to *Am I willing to risk regretting letting go of this old sweatshirt from my alma mater?* to *Am I willing to risk my friend being upset with me for giving away the ugly souvenir they brought me from Paraguay?* Consider what level and type of risk a given decision exposes you to and how you want to manage it when rationalizations and *what-ifs* arise. Better defining a given risk and expanding your risk tolerance in minimalism practice will be fruitful throughout this practice.

How do you control your tendency to rationalize material choices and prevent *what-ifs* ad nauseam? Acknowledge that you do this in the first place. Analyze common themes like scarcity mindset, never wanting to hurt someone's feelings, and hanging on to an aspirational identity. Observe when it happens in the moment: Does it cause you stress? Solidify a decision you've already made? Or perhaps even clarify your concerns? When you consider whether to keep or buy something, consider your *whys*, identities, status quo assumptions, and dedication to creating a minimalist lifestyle. It won't halt the rationalizing completely, but it will move you toward a more honest and strategic decision-making strategy.

Question all your rationalizations and *what-ifs*. Don't let these be the drivers of your decisions. Like your emotions, they are worth noting in your decision-making equation but are mostly just mental chatter emphasizing the unknown future and small risks in ways that don't matter as much as you think.

Questioning Organization, Optimization, and Productivity

The commonly desired outcomes of a minimalist life are perfectly organized physical and digital spaces, fully optimized life systems, and an emphasis on squeezing the most out of every minute through productivity. As a result, tools and strategies for superior organization, optimization, and productivity are often over-emphasized. However, the self-discovery work we've been doing has a more significant impact on your satisfaction and alignment with the minimalist lifestyle you're developing.

111

It's possible to get distracted by tactics or perfection if we're not careful. So let's look at how to apply organizing, optimization, and productivity while avoiding common misconceptions and pitfalls.

Organization and simplicity

While minimalism involves organizing, the goal is not to be the most organized. It's to organize with the least effort, in the most maintainable way, at the desired aesthetic base level to find what you need quickly and easily. We're all different, so different ways of organizing will get each person to this goal.

For example, you may be a visual person, either born from the joys of design or trying to avoid "out of sight, out of mind" syndrome. While the idyllic image of organized spaces is primarily bare walls and cleared surfaces, that's not the only way to do it. A bulletin board covered with beautiful postcards, a calendar, and other adornments may work for you, as may housing most of your kitchen gadgets on the countertop. These strategies can be a part of your organized space as long as it's purposeful and true to you. If you are a visual person, you don't have to conform. Trying to be someone you are not will cause discomfort, and you won't be able to create the minimalist lifestyle that is best for you.

I've found that people who don't have a natural proclivity toward organizing are more likely to over-organize in certain areas. They assume that's what they should do to be an organized person, or it's an unintentional overapplication of organizing strategies. It might be a result of trying to control things too much or a misunderstanding of how organizing works. How many categories and bins do you really need to find what you're looking for? It's only effective to the point of easy maintenance. Over-organization can waste time later when trying to maintain the organizational system created. Organize to the point that you're saving your future self time but no further.

For those who enjoy the experience of organizing and for the perfectionists out there, I can say that while I want to organize my digital files and notes to perfection, space out everything in my kitchen cabinets geometrically, and have all my clothes perfectly folded, I'd find myself slippery-sloping into diminishing returns. It's no longer serving the goal of a simple life. Admittedly, it's fun for me. And if it's truly fun for you, treat it as such and not a necessity.

Being super-duper-organized does not mean your life is simple. Organizing and simplifying are not synonymous. It's easy to mistake organization for simplicity because it's easier to organize than simplify, and the visual result of organization can *look* simple. Undoing complexity takes time, mental energy, and know-how, especially if you assume the complexity is necessary because it's always been there. But if you work with simplicity as your goal rather than organization, you'll have more efficient space and systems. The time saved in managing an efficient space and the joy it'll give you more than makes up for your efforts to simplify versus merely organize.

Imagine a bookshelf full of artfully arranged texts by color for visual appeal and delicately placed decorative items purchased purely for color coordination. Most people would look at that bookshelf and say it's organized. Organized for what? How does it help the person living there select a book off the shelf? The objects taking up space on the shelves aren't beloved or meaningful (unless purchased with great admiration). Some books may never be read, read again, or hold any special meaning because they weren't downsized. They were kept to ensure the bookshelf was full and had the right spectrum of colors.

The volume of books and the difficult-to-navigate color system is a missed opportunity for simplicity, efficiency, and meaning in deference to aesthetic organization. This is a basic example. There are far more unnecessary complexities and inefficiencies lurking in our offices, bedrooms, and garages. Many of which are less obvious.

Pay closer attention to whether your actions are meant to organize or simplify, you've considered the most efficient tactics, and your organizational efforts address what is most important and meaningful to you. Remember the words of author George Sand: "Simplicity is the most difficult thing to secure in this world; it is the last limit of experience and the last effort of genius." And Leonardo Da Vinci: "Simplicity is the ultimate sophistication."

Optimization

Like with organizing, we can hyper-focus on the goal of optimizing our lives while missing how best to apply optimizing strategies to gain the most benefit. Optimization should save us time and effort. It's the "get the most bang for your buck" mentality, but it should stop short of seeing it as a goal unto itself.

When you start to downsize and simplify, question how far to optimize something. Where do the diminishing returns appear? When is potential joy lost? When do you simply become a robot? Friction can be meaningful; it can be rich. We all need to space out and daydream and get lost in Google every once in a while. Identify the optimal optimization line for yourself.

Let's consider an example of optimizing effectively and avoiding potential pitfalls. I have a friend who pays to get his groceries delivered. His reasoning is simple: He doesn't like going to grocery stores, tends to buy mostly the same items weekly, and his professional hourly rate is higher than the delivery fee. Also, he's not bothered by one of the primary optimization systems fails: Ordered items are left out of the delivery, or the wrong ones are included. He doesn't care if the best cantaloupe isn't chosen. Further, he doesn't spend time continually trying all the grocery stores and shopping strategies to optimize. Instead, he found something that performed well enough and addressed the problem he wanted to solve. Grocery delivery wins when looking at the situation from all angles. It's optimization done right.

Optimization done wrong, on the other hand, happens when you invest a lot of time and money into a system to gain a small advantage. I see this most often with software. When we rely on multiple apps to do much of the work, things become murky: layers of to-do lists, calendars, automations, content curators, and reminders. We're left with work we don't expect like discovering overlap, system updates, and not noticing when the system breaks. Be careful not to let the pursuit of optimization become its downfall.

Productivity

Productivity faces the same cultural celebration and potential for diminishing returns that lead us away from the simple, meaningful minimalist lifestyle we're trying to attain. We must question productivity for productivity's sake ... but boy, do I love being productive! Are you with me? Checking things off a list. *Crossing everything off the list so you can throw away the list.* But if you go down the rabbit hole of productivity hacks, you'll find that they are mostly just hacks. Productivity can be buoyed a bit by tools, but mainly it's buoyed by mindset: Stay focused on your priorities, employing the least effort for the best outcome. Experiment with what works best for you. Be ready to switch gears if certain productivity strategies no longer help you or your priorities and you need to readjust your approach.

A common pitfall is getting distracted by reading books and articles about productivity and focus. This can be a time suck and may not result in you implementing any of the strategies. Or you do implement productivity strategies, but some require a time investment. Then, you may switch strategies when you hear about a new productivity system. When the focus becomes productivity itself, instead of what you want to do more efficiently and effectively, re-evaluate your approach. Have you crossed a tipping point where you're not optimizing your time anymore because the return on your investment is nil or costly? Here, contentment becomes challenging to achieve because there is always a sense of "I can be more productive" past the point of producing a significant result.

As mentioned with optimization, too much focus on productivity can result in a frictionless lifestyle. This may lead to you losing your patience and ability to deal with the unexpected moments of daily difficulties. Parts of your system not working perfectly may become problematic. It's easy to fall into the expectation of life working so smoothly that the smallest detours rock you. And you may even blame yourself for these, having fallen under the impression that you have much more control over your life than you do. Some friction helps us build strength and resilience. It lets us see that we don't (and shouldn't) have control over everything.

Every once in a while, I reflect on the only thing I recall from reading Robert M. Pirsig's book *Zen and the Art of Motorcycle Maintenance*. The narrator talks about how, when riding his motorcycle, getting to his destination isn't about making good time in the way that making good time is about getting somewhere faster. In his world, to "make good time" means that the time itself is good. Be productive, but make it good.

We need to get things done to accomplish what we want in life. The degree to which we can make that time more pleasant is worthwhile. Further, by using mindset change, working on things that matter to us, and creating the best home environment to execute our tasks, we can save time, keep it simple, and stay focused on our goals. While questioning how organization, optimization, and productivity fit into your minimalist lifestyle may seem premature before we delve into how to downsize, it's an impactful layer best considered at the beginning of your lifestyle development.

Do You Really Care About Your Stuff?

After questioning macro assumptions, analyzing various costs, and determining whether our rationalizations are valid, let's return to something more fundamental: Do you even care about your stuff?

Do you treat your things like junk? Do you leave things on the floor, tripping over or stepping on them, creating a nuisance on top of poor stewardship? Do you claim something is important while treating it as if it weren't? It's time to question whether how much you *think* you care about your things is matched by how you treat them and whether you're accumulating stuff you don't care about for the wrong reasons.

Consider whether you have an item because you care about it. It could be because of need (e.g., a car to get you from home to work), because you absolutely love it (e.g., a pair of jeans you wear all the time as they fit like a glove), or because it's meaningful to you (e.g., a letter from your late grandmother). If you care for any of these reasons, is your treatment of the item mirroring its importance? If not, not only is this hurting you (e.g., emotionally and possibly financially), but this is also an area where you are not aligned. It's much like saying your *why* for living with less is to align with your spiritual beliefs, yet you have an excess of stuff you could contribute to the less fortunate. Note these inconsistencies and begin to correct them.

For items you care about but aren't treating well, why? For example, do you leave indoor things outdoors or keep important objects in unlidded cardboard boxes in unconditioned spaces? Maybe you lacked the knowledge to care for them well. Maybe you thought what you were doing was enough. Maybe you lack education about some aspect of how to maintain things. Maybe you simply hate cleaning and tidying up. Be specific and honest in this investigation.

Next, consider whether it's an item you don't care about much but assume you do without thinking. Sometimes, we only "care" about something because we *own* it, so it feels natural to continue keeping it. Minimalism is a dissector of assumptions. Ask yourself whether this item is what you want to put your time, energy, and general care toward relative to other things in your life. If you don't treat it well, that may indicate that you took for granted that you cared about it, but its mistreatment highlights that this is not the case.

Consider how the way you treat your stuff relates to gratitude. When you contemplate your appreciation for your stuff, does it track with how you actively treat it? Question whether you are showing gratitude for what you have by treating it well. Conversely, ask yourself: If you treat your things like they mean nothing to you, why are you holding onto them so tightly? Or default to keeping them?

To drive the point of all this further, if your friend treated you like crap, would you feel like they cared about you? Explore how much you honestly care about your things and how this aligns with your actions. Are you being a lousy friend to your stuff? If you are, accidentally, do what you need to do to learn and make amends.

Undo Your Defaults, Open Doors

Everything is up for questioning. You're a "stuff interrogator" sitting across from each item or lifestyle choice, demanding to know its value, asking it the tough questions. We are in the decision-making process every time we take action, no matter how large or small. When we decide to make a quick purchase or add something to our calendars that distract us from our priorities, we are answering, by default, how we want minimalism to be integrated into our lives.

Becoming adept at asking the right questions will come in handy as you rebuild your mindset, as it opens new doorways in your mind and makes space for a new way of thinking.

Part IV

Rebuild Your Mindset

You've spent the last few parts of this book defining your *why* and values, removing identity barriers, questioning assumptions, and possibly uncovering something you didn't know about yourself. You've created a new foundation on which to build your minimalist mindset!

We all have a mindset. It's typically influenced by our values, the people we spend time with, our upbringing, and what we read and watch. Often, it's created passively, partly by views we hold but haven't consciously accepted. These frameworks heavily influence our life choices, so embarking on mindset change is paramount to an intentional life.

Suppose your mindset is that life is a nonstop hustle. In that case, you will always have too much to do. As a result, a peaceful lifestyle will elude you, as will more time freedom.

If you see the material world as representing success, wealth, or hard work, you will remain on the unsatisfying hamster wheel of accumulation. However, if you view material objects as tools to build a simple life, you're more likely to acquire high-quality objects to support your goals. Additionally, you'll enjoy more freedom by purchasing services and experiences with your extra funds.

If you inherited a mindset about what a home should look like through advertisements or your childhood home, you may have a narrow mindset about what a home "should" be. Do you need a television and couch in the living room? If you see a living room without those features as empty, that directly results from your mindset. Conversely, minimalism is a blank slate that doesn't limit us to the status quo.

If you grew up without financial security, you may have inherited a scarcity mindset that overemphasizes holding on, even when you have enough. It is often related to anxiety. Instead, a minimalist mindset includes an abundance mindset in which, at any moment, we can say, "I have enough."

How about helpful mindsets you may already have? For example, if you practice being present daily, you likely have a mindful mindset, which is integral to a minimalist approach. A mindful mindset values being in the moment and tapping into your true feelings. It helps us have perspective when we're struggling with *what-if* scenarios and identity issues that arise during the downsizing process.

Mindset change is the most effective path toward minimalism (and part of the brainwashing I mentioned in the How to Start chapter). We're jumpstarting your process in this book, but the depth and breadth of change can take years. Though, sometimes, parts of it can happen instantaneously.

Take fast fashion for example. Inexpensive but trendy clothing was, at first, seen mostly as harmless by the American mainstream. But when the 2013 collapse of the Rana Plaza garment factory in Bangladesh killed over one thousand workers, shoppers started to change their minds. And when the 2015 documentary *The True Cost* further exposed the dangerous impacts of the industry on its workers and our environment, it transformed the way many Americans viewed fast fashion. While this cultural mindset shift didn't cause a complete industry overhaul, many shoppers couldn't "unsee" what had been so vividly brought to their consciousness, and they began turning away from fast fashion, minimizing their purchases overall and opting for more sustainable shopping methods as their finances allowed.

Mindset change doesn't happen only through horrific tragedies or explosive documentaries. There are softer methods. Learning how to draw provides a helpful example of how a slightly different mindset can alter everything. *Drawing on the Right Side of the Brain*, by Betty Edwards, posits that anyone can draw well and that it's less a mechanical or creative skill and more of a seeing one. Drawing becomes infinitely more approachable and accurate when you shift to seeing lines and shapes instead of what you believe the object should look like. Everyone can draw. You just need to look at the world a bit differently.

In this section, I'll help you investigate your current mindsets and their influences by examining various factors such as ownership, decision-making, gratitude, guilt and shame, and delayed gratification. You'll see how shifting your mindset can influence your actions, and it's the simplest way to practice minimalism.

Vow to Be Honest

What does honesty have to do with minimalism?

Before you rebuild your mindset, ensure you're doing it from a truthful place and that it's the first level you begin rebuilding. It is the basis from which we view the world and how we interact with it. Also, how often you tell little lies to others and yourself that relate to your material possessions and lifestyle might surprise you. These can add up and take us off course from the alignment you're attempting to achieve. If you aren't honest, you will struggle more with establishing your minimalist mindset and all the decision-making ahead of you.

Not being truthful to others about your needs and preferences can result in receiving and keeping things you don't want and cause the connection you have with others to be less authentic. Honesty is necessary to ensure that the lifestyle you want doesn't give way to the desire to seem more well-off or put together to others via material accumulation. Generally, lying to yourself about who you are and what you want creates a lifestyle that isn't sincere.

Minimalism, in many ways, is truth. It breaks down who you are, your values, and what you like and need. Most people think they're honest and that honesty is a core value. But much like mindfulness, we aren't as honest as we think we are, so taking a vow to try to be as honest as you can during this process is paramount to your success.

But the occasional white lie is okay, right? Only lying to be nice and prevent someone from feeling bad is doing them a favor, right?

It can be, but not typically.

White lies are like being a little pregnant. White lies are still lies. Not that we need to eradicate them completely; however, we must own up to them and then consider why we chose a white lie as the best solution. I'm not referring to white lies that pop up in extreme cases where there is a selfless and profound reason. More along the lines of white lying to your coworker who gives you yet another bobblehead even though you already have four others from them. And you hate bobbleheads.

Someone once told me that a really good friend is someone who'll tell you when you have mustard on your cheek while eating a sandwich. It's oddly uncomfortable to point out to them, but it allows your friend to wipe it away before embarrassing themself in front of others (even if they feel a bit embarrassed when you point it out).

Often, the impetus for a white lie (or outright lie) is to avoid experiencing how *you* will feel when the other person is potentially upset by the truth. This tends to be the driver for the lie, but we rationalize that it was for the other person's sake. It's a genuinely unsettling feeling to tell the truth sometimes. It's human to avoid discomfort. We fear judgment and don't like being perceived in any way that we don't want. We may pass it off as being too preoccupied to deal with the issue, but minimalism is all about finally dealing with everything and creating new habits.

We often keep and gift items because we fear being honest. We don't want to attend a party without a gift because we think it's expected of us, even though it may go against our values. We hold onto a family member's storage because we don't want them to think we're selfish, even as we try to downsize our homes. We resist letting people know we don't like material gifts for our birthday because we're afraid it'll hurt their feelings.

One of the most significant problems with lying is that it is a means to control someone else's experience or reality. It's an unintended manipulation, but it's not fair to them. Lies are a crutch when we are not calling upon our strength or smarts to resolve the situation without them. More honesty can build resilience.

Keep in mind that being honest and oversharing aren't synonymous. Nor does being honest necessarily involve brutal directness. There is a place in between. On the other side, there are lies of omission. These can typically be identified when you break out technicalities, trying to convince yourself that it's not a lie.

Then, there's the lying we do with ourselves. We want to be

someone we are not, either through what we own, what we buy, or the activities we partake in. Also, the truth for you can change over time, so we must be mindful of when we change but our stuff and routines don't. Lying to ourselves can happen when we want to believe that we haven't changed or that our relationships with others haven't changed. What's true isn't always straightforward.

Our culture assumes and expects a level of dishonesty, so you may not notice how much it's a part of your life. It makes assessing your honesty more complicated, but it will pay off as you can apply minimalism more efficiently during the downsizing process and while maintaining your new minimalist lifestyle.

Behavioral Economics and Common Biases

We need to understand how our minds may play tricks on us to rebuild our mindsets. We can't change our minds effectively if we don't understand them. For instance, sometimes, we act and make decisions against our best interests. To help us figure out why, behavioral economics emerged. This field of study addresses how people act in a system and how our actions counter what would otherwise be considered logical. We have biases that we don't choose to have, but they influence our thinking and our actions with little awareness. Our attempts at rationality trip over these processing errors caused by us simply being human.

While we can't always prevent them, we can identify when these biases emerge and how they affect our choices (and how we apply minimalism to our lives). These tendencies are latent, so their excavation is at the beginning of our rebuilding process.

I've found that the following behavioral biases appear when we struggle with ownership, decision-making, and emotional reactions, all of which are minimalism-related. Think of this as a glossary and identify which are relevant to your experience with downsizing:

Decision Fatigue: The psychological costs of decision-making. It can lead to poor choices or a diminished ability to exercise self-control. Often, my clients know 75 percent of what they need to do, but the experience of sitting in their chaos, making decision after decision, knocks their progress off course.

Endowment Effect: When people overvalue something they own, regardless of its objective market value. I notice the endowment effect when people are almost ready to let something go, but when they realize no one will buy it or give them "what it's worth," they end up holding onto it. (Not talking about expensive collector's items or items with a known market value that only require the right buyer.) It's one thing to keep something you think you may use but another to recognize that you're ready to let it go and keep it anyway.

Hedonic Adaptation: People get used to life changes and then return to a relatively stable level of happiness despite major positive or adverse events; for example, when someone gets a promotion and experiences excitement, believing it will improve their life. Then, it becomes the norm, and they return to the level of happiness they had before the promotion. This happens when people believe that specific material objects will solve their problems, making them happier or less stressed. This is rarely the result.

Hyperbolic Discounting: Also known as "present bias." When people prefer smaller, immediate rewards over larger, later rewards; for example, when you impulse-buy an expensive item today instead of putting the money in a savings account for a dream vacation.

IKEA Effect: When the work you invested (e.g., the blood, sweat, tears, and missing pieces involved in building IKEA furniture) leads to the inflated value attributed to an item. It might come from the positive feelings of successfully completing the task or simply liking something you put effort into. This can happen when you spend much time and effort researching a particular product. You have more positive feelings associated with it because of the effort, which may make it difficult to let go of when you no longer need it.

Loss Aversion: People dislike losses more than an equivalent gain. In other words, giving up something is more painful than the pleasure we get from receiving it. People are more willing to take risks to avoid a loss than to acquire a gain. When there is a *what-if* scenario predicted to be painful if a possession is relinquished, loss aversion takes control.

Opportunity Cost: The potential forgone profit when an alternative was chosen instead. Living a "non-minimalist" lifestyle is fundamentally an unrecognized opportunity cost. By stumbling along in the status quo, a more aligned and enjoyable use of your time and money (aka minimalist lifestyle) is lost.

Projection Bias: When people think their preferences won't change, whether short- or long-term, because of changes in tastes. Projection bias may have led you to invest in expensive gym equipment for your home, assuming you'd always use it. Then you're stuck with an item you no longer use once you become a Pilates class addict. The sunk cost fallacy (see below) is in full effect.

Regret Aversion: Fear that your decision will turn out to be wrong in hindsight. Much like our *what-ifs*, we're so scared of regret that we don't see how the remorse over letting go of our old keychain collection is not as bad as routinely re-evaluating whether we still want to keep them and letting them contribute to the sea of stuff in our homes that weigh us down. Fear that you might be wrong is not necessarily a reason to keep something, especially when such a decision is rarely "wrong or right."

Sunk Cost Fallacy: When people make decisions today about previously invested time and resources. The more you invest in something (whether it's money or time), the harder it is to let go. It's similar to an IKEA effect but more common with money than effort. For example, if you decide to get into photography and buy a bunch of camera equipment but ultimately realize you don't enjoy it, pushing yourself to learn photography or keeping the supplies in the hopes you will *later* or beating yourself up about it ignores the sunk cost fallacy.

Which of these relate most to your challenges? Note how they show up when you try to make purchases or let go of things. The more you keep these behavioral biases in mind, the easier it will be to course-correct and rebuild a new way of thinking.

Unpacking Ownership

We touched on the challenges with ownership in the Behavioral Economics and Common Biases chapter with the endowment effect (overvaluing something we own, regardless of its objective market value). That tends to happen when we consciously want to keep something and it's valuable, sentimentally or financially. But ownership extends to anything in our homes or spaces we have authority over, regardless of whether we wanted it there in the first place or how minor its importance. We must address all items, big or small, purchased or free, to explore the mindset of ownership.

Once an item passes your front door, the tentacles of control slowly emerge. It is now *your* stuff. You own various things from, say, a marketing flyer, to the vitamin sample they gave at the grocery store, to the new sweater you just bought. You find yourself with an unintended responsibility for everything: whether it stays or goes and/or where to put it. It's a quick turn of circumstance that mostly happens unintentionally.

When it comes to items we didn't purchase or seek out, it's like our homes need their own bouncers just to manage the influx. From accepting all gifts (whether desired or not), to hand-me-downs out of guilt, to freebies that flood in, to unwanted mail, much of what we own wasn't invited. We don't think much of it when a singular item gets passed along to us. Then, unexpectedly, it becomes something hard to let go of or to decide what to do with, so you let it stay where it is by default.

In the case of items you purchase, like a set of dish towels, you may have loved them at first but then realized they weren't absorbent enough. You never reach for them and end up purchasing different ones. The first set lingers in a drawer. Now what?

You become attached to the stories about these unintended or minor objects (e.g., I really should take these vitamins; I need to get healthy!). Attachment can be quick and sticky. When we resist letting go because of attachment, we haven't questioned why we have this stuff to begin with and why, honestly, we feel the need to keep it. This is, in part, why we end up with more than we need.

When you're ready to loosen your grip, you may say, "I can do without this. But surely someone else will love it just as I did! It's such a wonderful thing!" You're ready to part ways but not until you know who the receiver will be or at least that there is a worthy receiver ready to use these items. This attempt to control an object beyond your ownership tightens your grip.

There is a distinction between control and responsibility. Once you let an item, big or small, pass your threshold, you make an informal agreement to oversee it. Where it goes next is your responsibility. So you must balance not letting things into your home that you don't want to be responsible for and loosening the grip on items you own but may need to let go of.

Become the tough bouncer and, when it's time to let go, really let go. Unpacking what "ownership" is results in a mindset shift. Ultimately, you want to own your life, not your stuff. Often, it's the other way around.

Stop Accepting Adult Homework

Are you still accepting homework assignments as an adult? I consider "adult homework assignments" relatively small things you don't want to do but find yourself responsible for completing at someone's direct or indirect request. These tasks cause you to ask, "How is this on my to-do list?!" Often, we've accepted them without full awareness or to avoid feeling guilty. Along with rejecting identities imposed upon you by others, eschewing unwelcome homework assignments, especially as they pertain to material items, is part of setting boundaries and being honest with yourself and others.

Often, adult homework assignments first seem like things that require minimal effort. But seemingly effortless tasks can gnaw at you, keep moving from list to list, and incrementally add up to mild annoyance, distraction, and resentment.

In my TEDx Talk, *The Darker Side of Gift Giving*, I explain how a gift, when not wholly desired, often becomes an adult homework assignment. It may carry more guilt, especially when navigating social norms about gift expectations. What do you do with this gift now? You didn't agree to a task per se, but in accepting the gift, you have the task of deciding what to do with it and then following through.

Then there's gift-giving's more insidious cousin: unintentional receiving. Unintentional receiving is often perpetrated through freebies, food someone brings into your home, and hand-me-downs. These may be someone pawning off *their* guilt of getting rid of something that they would otherwise trash or have to figure out how to get rid of. They try to earn feel-good points by giving it to you and save themselves from further decision-making. They've passed that responsibility along to you.

Imagine your friend brings something into your home unexpectedly and thinks (pretends?) they're doing you two favors: offering something for free that you might like and letting you off the hook up front by saying, "You don't need to keep it. You can do whatever you want with it, and I won't be offended." Now you have this object in your home that you don't really want. After they leave, you most likely will ignore it at first because it's not a priority. It's yours now, so it's just … here. If you accepted it without thinking it through, you'll eventually have to decide whether it's worth keeping and, if so, where to put it and, if not, decide what to do with it (i.e., add another adult homework assignment to your list).

I'm not suggesting you never do a favor for someone or that unintentional receiving is always a problem. Minimalism provides you with newfound time and focus to do more for people you care about, as long as you're clear about when you want to do a favor and when it's best to decline the task, the gift (respectfully), or the unintentionally received object.

Your new minimalist mindset involves being more aware of how you spend your time and becoming more honest. Adult homework assignments will pull you in the opposite direction, potentially leaving you with more objects in your home. Recognize when these assignments are presented so you can make a conscious decision about what you want to do about them. Find a balance between helping others and being kind while being intentional about your efforts.

The Fleeting Glee Trap

You make a purchase. You go home and open it: place it on display, put it on, use it. This feels great because you wanted it. You may have wanted it for a long time, building the anticipation. Maybe it was finally on sale, or you just *had* to have it.

This momentary sense of glee makes you think you made a great choice. It's a feeling you would like to replicate. While fleeting, you associate the positive feeling with the object long after the emotion has subsided. Or in some cases, you continue looking at, wearing, or using the object, still experiencing additional moments of joy, though less intense.

Your good feeling is not the problem. The problem occurs when you unconsciously associate it with meaning. You risk forming a mindset focused on fleeting, superficial happiness rather than the purposefulness we're aiming to build our lifestyles on. As a result, we may justify shopping more to experience those joyful moments repeatedly. We may put aside our whys and values in deference to a superfluous, expensive pair of sunglasses. If you give these good feelings a misplaced weight, your decision-making will be skewed toward instant gratification.

Giving significance and meaning to a momentary sense of glee may mean that you're not considering the hedonic treadmill. The hedonic treadmill is our proclivity to quickly return to our typical level of happiness regardless of major positive (or negative) events in our lives.[4] It's like the hedonic adaptation discussed in the Behavioral Economics and Common Biases chapter. We spend most of our lives at a particular happiness set point that remains the norm despite all events, big and small. This includes our purchasing decisions. The sense of satisfaction is fleeting or retreating, but we tend to overemphasize these positive feelings and use them to rationalize our purchases. We must be careful not to overvalue them and their overall effect on our happiness level.

This doesn't mean you can't buy something for fun or that it's shallow to appreciate and enjoy some material items. Instead, develop the discernment that Meaningful Minimalism offers. If you need a sweater, you might as well love it and be excited about it. Embrace the excitement you feel when you first wear it, and let it be fleeting. But understand the difference between the joy of a

---

4 Brickman and Campbell coined the term in their essay "Hedonic Relativism and Planning the Good Society" (1971).

new mattress that will help your back problem versus a new watch. Grow a greater appreciation for each purchase, especially as you now see that you don't "deserve" it.

When developing a minimalist lifestyle predicated on meaning, we can pay closer attention to the types and depths of happiness we experience. They might not be the same as when we've researched for months for the best new earphones and finally got them. Having meaning and fulfillment in your life doesn't feel the same as the high you get from material purchases. Once you have something or have achieved something, you get used to it, and the thrill (typically) is gone. Double-check with yourself when you base decisions on that rush of glee instead of reminding yourself of the pitfalls of the hedonic treadmill.

Play with Delayed
Gratification

The fleeting glee trap we just investigated is closely related to instant gratification. Instant gratification is our cultural currency and is likely a contributor to why you have more stuff than you need. It's that hit of dopamine we seek out, regardless of the consequences. Instead of chasing the rush, you can develop a mindset that emphasizes delayed gratification. Patience, through the experience of delayed gratification, is a seldom-explored avenue to experience life's pleasures.

Opening the box from an online order, or even the impulse to make the online purchase itself, is riddled with consequences we ignore in pursuit of immediate excitement. As we develop our minimalist lifestyle, we must ask ourselves tough questions. For example, does the purchase align with our priority of saving money to pay off debt and reduce stress? If not, why did we purchase it?

Instant gratification is not limited to shopping. It may also pop up when accepting gifts and freebies that thrill us initially but leave us with too much stuff or tasks. The mood lift passes quickly.

Instant gratification even comes up in the organizing process, or at least how people experience it on social media. While I've heard repeatedly that I should share before and after photos of spaces I've organized to advertise my business, it promotes instant gratification that can do a disservice to this work. When viewing a photo of an overwhelmingly cluttered space, a rush of pleasure follows when seeing the problem immediately fixed. Both the quick fix and the aesthetic of the finished closet alone are enticing. But where did the items go? What was the experience and process? It's the rush of instant gratification, without the work, that's being sought. No learning, no growing.

If we're moving away from instant gratification, we must replace it with delayed gratification. Delayed gratification supports the idea that feeling gratified is not as important as we think but that when we experience it, we can be more appreciative of it. If something is important to you, it can wait. It's the proverbial journey versus the destination.

You likely have delayed gratification when planning a trip or buying concert tickets in advance. You get the joys of planning and anticipation and, hopefully, a greater appreciation of the experience once it happens. If you've worked on a big personal project or large-scale assignment at work, it probably required visualization and an understanding of a somewhat malleable end product. It required patience and faith. Was the delayed payoff satisfying? You likely had meaningful learning experiences along the way, and the gratification was more textured and enriching than, say, receiving that new air fryer. The satisfaction is fully earned.

Appreciating delayed gratification makes us frugal when moving an item into a virtual cart but not immediately checking out. Perhaps, instead, we save up over a more extended period for an item that will be more special and impactful in our lives. Then, we can celebrate our resolve to be patient enough to get something we really want. From the lifestyle perspective, it enables us to persist through difficult times in relationships. The excitement of newness dissipates into a deeper connection. We develop trust and love over time.

Develop an acute awareness of how instant and delayed gratification occurs in different areas of your life. With delayed gratification, you'll not only have the benefits of fewer instant gratification-provoked purchases, but you'll also develop a new type of contentment. Delayed gratification is not only the antidote to instant gratification, it is also the foundation for a meaningful life.

The Preference Trap

We examined whether you care about your stuff and what you only *think* you care about in the Do You Really Care About Your Stuff? chapter. Now, as you rebuild your mindset, we need to find a sweet spot between caring enough and not caring too much. This balance will allow us to be respectful and grateful for what we have but not overvalue or get distracted by stuff. To determine where we care too much, we must investigate the *preference trap*. Then, we can adjust our mindset to calibrate the balance of caring.

Let's say you love getting a bagel before work and almost exclusively eat an everything bagel with cream cheese. But this morning, the last everything bagel was purchased by the person in front of you while you were checking your phone to see that you were already late for work. You see that there is poppyseed, which is okay, but you find yourself filled with acute irritation and a woe-is-me attitude. What are you supposed to do?

As much as poppy is barely a substitute for everything, your internal response is outsized. But moments like these can serve as insightful reminders that our preferences can control us, having too great a weight in our lives. This is a reason to catch ourselves, laugh, and start to build greater awareness.

Obedience to preference is why we acquire so much stuff and keep multiple versions of the same thing. We make slightly different choices in different situations, so we prepare ourselves with the specific products to support these distinctions. We also like to have variations of things because they offer us small and particular advantages (e.g., six different spatula sizes and shapes). Sometimes, those nuances make us feel clever for recognizing and valuing these details. We may even want others to notice and appreciate the things we adore and how they connect to our preferences and, therefore, our identities.

Having preferences isn't inherently problematic. It's when we reach the minutiae of distinctions with diminishing returns that we find ourselves going down a rabbit hole. As products continue to "improve," and options increase endlessly, we overemphasize nuanced differences rather than flexibility. Pursuing precisely what you want involves more time and money than not. With time, you can endlessly research the right product to fit your exact desire. With money, you can purchase more than you need and, possibly, more expensive items with more specific features. We can get lost in a tailspin of details and forget what's most important to us.

This leads to being too focused on "getting just what I want." We let preferences lead and prioritize them too much, feeling less satisfied when we don't have exactly what we want. If we appreciate what we have and what is right in front of us (e.g., a poppyseed bagel), we can avoid a sense of entitlement. Getting your preference is great but not necessary.

If you're unsure how attached you are to your preferences, try ignoring your preferences for a day and simply go with the flow. See what happens. If you want a particular item, don't get it, even if you can. See what it feels like to desire something and then let it go. Train yourself to be okay with that and enjoy the freedom it allows.

To adopt Meaningful Minimalism, we have to be mindful of the preference trap. While still caring for things that we genuinely desire, we can't let too much of our attention and money lead us down preference rabbit holes. Make sure you're finding balance in how much you care about your stuff and your preferences.

Curate Your Toolbox

The corollary to the preference trap is to identify which things (that you prefer) can make up your life's toolbox. All the stuff we hold in our homes, as well as our modes of transportation, money, and skills, are tools for experiencing life. When you begin the downsizing and organizing process, you'll choose which tools you want to keep, bring in, or let go. When you begin to see everything as a tool, it becomes easier to determine whether you need something and whether it'll help you live your values, priorities, and goals.

We use the word *tool* typically to describe fix-it devices: products with the sole purpose of manipulating a thing to make it better or no longer broken. We all know that the tool doesn't do all the work. The tool enables the work to be done more easily and better. Choosing the right tool is extremely important. A hammer can drive in a nail in just the right spot or be used as a weapon. In this way, all your possessions are tools (not just your hammer and screwdriver).

Through the "tool" lens, you'll question the functions of all the items you own. We take many household items for granted because we assume we need them. And if we have them, we tend to use them somehow, even if it's not what's best for us. Instead, if we take the tool approach, we can ask ourselves whether a particular kitchen appliance is fixing or improving something. What function does it serve, and can that function, if needed, be served by a different tool? It's easier to adopt this mindset with items in the kitchen or office, but what about furniture, hobby supplies, pieces of art, or sentimental objects? Ask yourself: What purpose does this serve? What goal will it help me reach? Does it align with my values?

This doesn't mean that a possession with a sentimental or historical purpose no longer has a place, but the questions surrounding whether it should be kept can become more sophisticated. No one would choose a tool to make them sad or guilty, but perhaps a sentimental item is a tool to connect with a loved one who has passed. Much like only needing one or two hammers, you only need a few items to forge that relationship connection in the material world.

This approach encourages repurposing items rather than trashing them. If each item is a tool, you can choose the function it serves. Even something as simple as an old toothbrush can become a grout scrubber. A toothbrush is a tool for cleaning teeth or tiles—your choice. Tools with multiple purposes prevent us from buying more and unnecessarily specific items. Focusing on functionality is the basis for understanding whether something adds a benefit.

Your skills and personality traits are tools too. There are no good or bad traits, just tools that can be helpful or harmful, depending on their use. Perhaps you are adept at time management and planning. These are undeniably useful skills, but they can be harmful if you allow them to make you rigid, lose sight of the big picture, or close you off to spontaneous adventures.

If everything is a tool, then religions, philosophies, self-help systems, and even minimalism are tools. Any type of lifestyle approach is a tool to accomplish a given goal. They can be used well or miss the point entirely.

Once the toolbox mindset shift occurs, it's easier to see what you need to keep and what you're lacking. It trains you to ask questions about the value of something and its purpose from a functionality perspective. As a bonus, this shift prevents you from treating ideas, personality traits, and objects as good or bad. It removes judgment.

Transform Guilt into Gratitude

Guilt and shame often emerge when I help clients downsize. Sometimes, they feel so much shame about their state of affairs that it's difficult for them to let me in their home, even though my purpose is to help them undo the very distress that led them to call me in the first place. The emotional weight of guilt and shame will paralyze your minimalist efforts, or you'll hobble through them painfully, ineffectively, and sometimes overdramatically. So we've got to deal with it.

While this book is not meant to be a therapy session on the sources and manifestations of all your guilt and shame, you'll begin to investigate where your guilt and shame come from and where it's a barrier to this work. Then, you can transform it into something positive, like gratitude, and begin to let it go.

I can tell you from being in terribly dirty, completely disorganized homes, where the inhabitants regularly miss bill payments, have rotten food in the fridge, and lose important items ... there is nothing to be ashamed of. These are all physical manifestations of internal problems that haven't been solved yet. We all have internal problems, but not all of them have such "shameful" physical outputs.

As vulnerability researcher Brené Brown says, "Shame is a focus on self, guilt is a focus on behavior. Shame is 'I am bad.' Guilt is 'I did something bad.'" In relation to minimalism, guilt is a reason people keep stuff they don't want or need and why their to-do lists and calendars are overrun by undesired commitments. Social mores and cultural expectations gear up our guilt.

When we keep something out of guilt, it may be because it was an heirloom, and we would feel guilty to let it go. Or we may feel guilty with respect to the responsibility we hold for others, like, "I feel so bad about throwing away my kids 'drawings' from when they were five. Is that wrong? What if they want them later?" Taken a step further into shame... "Am I a terrible mom???"

When we feel guilty, it may be prompted by a belief that we are unworthy of having more than others (even if we're not the reason why they have less, aka "did something bad"). Does this guilt help anyone? It certainly doesn't help the people who have it worse than you. Sometimes, we feel guilty about letting go of things in a way that is misaligned with reality. For example, we feel guilty when throwing something in the trash we no longer want, even when that's the only remaining option for that item. Unpacking the origin of the guilt and which values it connects to will help loosen its grip.

In addition to becoming aware of it and why you're experiencing it, practicing gratitude can help you let it go. Guilt can be thought of as the negative side of gratitude. Sometimes, we are so aware of how lucky we are that we emotionally go overboard and let it turn into guilt. Before allowing our good fortune to become negative, we can adopt some pragmatism to let go of things we don't need and feel more appreciative about what we keep. We can reap gratitude.

Gratitude practices, like keeping a gratitude journal, help people step outside of themselves and their daily challenges to recognize how fortunate they are. But it's only the first step. It's what you do with that gratitude that ultimately matters. Gratitude should not be a momentary emotion or intellectualized feeling that's briefly acknowledged and put aside. Instead, use it as a doorway to form a deeper understanding of our interconnectedness, a way of slowing down, and a moment of mindfulness.

How can you move beyond feeling grateful in a moment and take action? For example, reframe the guilt of buying something you don't need as a reminder to feel grateful that you had the funds to buy such a thing in the first place and that this "mistake purchase" was a great lesson to learn and an opportunity to give to someone in need.

If we keep things in our homes that we're not using, we're not being helpful to the people who gave them to us (that's just guilt), the environment (if it has to go in the trash eventually), or people in need (thinking you *should* keep something because others have less than you). It may at first feel like we're not being wasteful when keeping things. But instead, we're preventing others from enjoying these items.

Revisiting what you questioned in the Do You Really Care About Your Stuff? chapter, if you treat your stuff poorly, are you grateful for it? If you are, can you turn that gratitude into action by treating what you decide to own in a more thoughtful manner? You can reflect on how you want to find the sweet spot between what you care about and how you want to experience gratitude.

When we truly feel grateful for our relationships, the money we make (or are given), the stuff we own, gifts, and all our opportunities, there is no room for guilt to stay. We can let go of others' expectations and use our resources to help those in need. While feelings will always arise, sometimes unexpectedly, we can acknowledge them and follow up with action. Don't just say you are grateful; act like you are grateful.

Letting go of guilt and shame from your life is a more significant project of which minimalism is only a part. Here, we're analyzing how we attach guilt and shame specifically to the current state of our home and life organization and how this stalls or distracts us. Guilt and shame bog us down and often lead to dishonesty. Gratitude lifts us so we can pivot and treat our possessions, relationships, and opportunities with the respect that gratitude brings. Repurpose what you used to feel guilty about as a pathway to add more goodness into the world.

Stop Pretending
Forever Exists

You're going to die.

Hopefully, not before you apply minimalism to your life so the person who has to go through your possessions has an easier time. But it will end, and most of us have no idea when. It's challenging to plan for the future and acknowledge that many of the future-dependent decisions you make about your stuff may not come to pass. That's why we need to give less weight to the future in ways that don't support our aligned lifestyles.

Planning for the future is prudent when the consequences of not planning are potentially dire. If you don't save for retirement or have insurance, you might find yourself hopelessly indebted, bankrupt, achingly poor, or homeless. Sometimes, attention to these *laters* is overlooked because of the time horizon, ignorance of the risks involved, or simply because they're not fun. While these are the most extreme and consequential *laters*, we'll put them aside to address more common *laters* related to the downsizing process.

The Layers of *Laters*

Your old college textbooks are still in the garage because you put off going through them until *later*. That was three years ago. Sometimes, putting it off means not prioritizing over other tasks or not having the bandwidth or knowledge to proceed. If you're being honest with yourself, you'll be able to determine whether that's the case or if the allure of *later* has manifested as a classic procrastination technique. It's easy to say, "I'll go through that box later," or "I'll get myself organized later," so we don't think much about it. Later may happen but not at a time that's convenient for you. Often, the careful review you anticipated will give way to a time crunch or more distractions. Deprioritizing or procrastinating can have negligible impact or unintended consequences. Either way, we need to determine whether these tasks must be taken care of right away or acknowledge that we'll never want to do them or keep track of them as future tasks.

Then, there are the *laters* where you've already decided to keep something, thinking that you'll have more time later to use it or because you're convinced you might need it later. Essentially, you're keeping items almost by default to support these predictions. But if you've turned your home into a storage unit, all for these *laters*, you don't have a home with the tools you need for today. You have unrealized promises to yourself.

Here's a seemingly logical explanation I get from clients: "I don't want to give that away because even though I haven't used it in six years, it's only because things are so busy. When things slow down later, I'll use it. Plus, I don't want to have to buy it again." That's not a lie. However, it's one of those rationalizations we discussed earlier. I don't want you to buy anything again either, but first, investigate whether it's as important to you as you think, whether the item is irreplaceable, or what the replacement cost is. Avoid taking this type of *later* for granted.

Sometimes our *laters* are proactive in nature, like when we buy something we aren't going to use now. As discussed in the The Hidden Costs of Stuff chapter, we make assumptions about our future selves being just like our past selves with our purchasing habits. We think we save money and gain convenience with larger-quantity purchases. Occasionally we do, but mostly not. Sometimes, we buy something for a project we're not ready to start. This may happen because an item is on sale, or we momentarily became excited by an idea. You might purchase an *Auto Repair for Dummies* book for when you finally have time to learn how to fix your car. But why buy it before being ready to take action? *Later* becomes a latent hope or a reason to be disappointed in ourselves.

Sometimes, these purchases are much bigger and more consequential. For example, my client Anna bought a brand-new mid-sized sedan in her early twenties. She lived in the city, drove infrequently, and was single. She assumed she'd soon get married and have kids, and she would "grow into" the car. She wasn't dating anyone at the time. A dozen years passed before she got married, bought a house, and had a kid. Now, she's discussing purchasing a different car to suit their current life. She made a big purchase for a *later* that may not have occurred, and it coming to fruition so much later than expected means that she should have made a more practical purchase initially.

We also feed our aspirational identities with *laters*. We might decide to keep that stack of empty notebooks for later when we decide to journal every day. Or we carry heavy emotional weight, like unrealized dreams we believe will finally get their due "someday." In getting caught up with our histories, we may use our futures as a crutch. In that way, we may continue to put off what we should address today.

Later Isn't in Our Control

All *laters* come with many assumptions, including significant ones like your future relationship status or the idea that your health will not have declined by the time you can finally take up snowboarding. I've seen this happen routinely. And occasionally, in more extreme circumstances. One client, Gemma, was diagnosed with multiple sclerosis in her late thirties, and by the time I began working with her, she was a wheelchair user. She experienced the grief of letting go of things she kept for a *later* that she would not be able to enjoy. Her neurological challenges, in addition to worsening sleep, lethargy, and nausea, required an evolving set of solutions. We had to be more thoughtful about short-term and long-term planning. It's not that all our expectations about the future are unreasonable and we can't plan for less likely outcomes, but we can begin to acknowledge these assumptions, at minimum.

Aside from specific ailments, aging affects what we can do and how we view what we own. As we get older, we begin to think more about our legacies. Sometimes this is born from a fear of mortality, a sudden, shivering concern that we haven't done enough to earn our right on this planet or as a way of holding onto our things. The idea of legacy permeates our thinking, adding another layer to future-focused decision-making that does little to simplify our lives today.

We begin to devise ways to live eternally. We want to believe that our stuff and our homes are a limb of our legacy and that others will be as interested in sorting through our material-based pasts as we hope. Unless you are Frank Lloyd Wright, your home is not your legacy. Your wisdom and kind words and the relationships you've formed are. The time you chose someone who needed consoling over going out to party. The time you said something so funny, it still makes your loved ones laugh. It's the things that make you uniquely you.

If you are in your third act and have stuff that you plan to leave to loved ones, ask yourself, "Can I give it to them now?" Think about whether you have a use for it now or if it would be most impactful to them at the present time. My client Martha is in her seventies and recently began giving away her jewelry collection. Not her favorite pieces but ones she doesn't wear anymore. Piece by piece, she tells the recipient the story of how the jewelry came into her possession. She's finding joy in the process. It is also a kindness because the person in charge of parsing her estate will have less work to do.

Even if you are decades away from this giveaway strategy, there is value in considering how the future unwinds. While we don't want to acknowledge our own mortality, we also avoid thinking about what this means for those we leave behind. If we keep pretending that the future exists, it's easy not to acknowledge that we're going to die, and while that means we will never have to organize our sock drawer again, it leaves a big responsibility for those close to us.

Perhaps you can, instead, leave a legacy of caring responsibility for yourself and others. Develop a mental filter to sort through the different types of *laters* to begin untethering yourself from empty promises, problematic assumptions, and unrealistic expectations. When your home space reflects this new reality, you will, in turn, become more present.

Decision-Making as a Skill

We seemingly make hundreds of decisions in a day. Each decision takes a bit of mental (and sometimes emotional) energy and time and the ability to see the big picture. We suffer from decision fatigue because we have to make so many decisions. The more we make, the harder it becomes to make them well.

Decision-making is not a skill most of us learn in school or as a hobby, and it's difficult to discern what constitutes excellent decision-making. While we'll discuss practical approaches to combat decision fatigue in the Combat Decision Fatigue chapter in Part 6, we'll start here by developing a better decision-making mindset. This will help you make more aligned and quicker decisions during the downsizing process and is a skill that you can apply to everything in your life.

To begin, identify the ingrained assumptions about whether you're a good decision-maker, whether you like making decisions, and how fast you are at making them. These assumptions are likely based on the type of situation. You may be swift and confident when making big decisions about your career and choosing a partner but flail when faced with picking out a new pair of jeans. We often need to further investigate these ingrained assumptions and the specific challenges we face in this arena.

The challenges we face when making choices abound. Difficulty stems from a lack of clarity about our goals, priorities, and values. Overarching decisions aren't made in lieu of treating each decision individually, creating more confusion. We get caught up in the notion that there are "right and wrong" decisions. We may delay or abandon making a decision out of fear of making the wrong one. Or spend excessive time deciding, assuming it'll decrease the chance of making a mistake. We forget that the outcome of most decisions is almost impossible to predict.

We don't know ourselves well enough to know what we want or need or how we feel about something. Or we get so caught up in the feelings of the choice rather than using feelings as one data point in logical decision-making. Sometimes, we focus too much on pragmatism and forget about how we feel inside. We don't know how to apply risk assessment to decisions that seem risky. Also, life offers more options and availability than ever before, so we're often faced with an overwhelming number of choices.

With all these challenges, it's no wonder that deciding which to-do list app to use or whether to keep that extra pair of socks we bought mistakenly can drive us crazy at times. Even those of us who enjoy more confident decision-making, along with the sense of control it offers, can still use a decision vacation. Along with your internal interrogation of decision-making proclivities, we'll reframe how you view choice, the right/wrong dichotomy, and trade-offs.

There is always a choice

Adopting the perspective that there is always a choice is foundational. While I don't want this to overwhelm you, it opens doors that may have felt closed. If it isn't evident yet, I'm trying to drive the point home that you have agency in your life that you've given away to others, systems, and cultural norms.

Please take this perspective at face value as it pertains to minimalism and daily decision-making, not philosophically. While we don't have much choice as it pertains to large-scale things like laws and the weather, we choose whether to follow the laws or not. We choose how we react and whether to grab an umbrella or get soaked in the rain.

In Viktor Frankl's book *Man's Search for Meaning*, about his experience surviving the Holocaust, he posits that even in the harshest of circumstances, where there are almost no choices we could call our own, we still have the choice of how we want to react, deal with, and perceive those circumstances. And that's where an inch of freedom lies.

Our life circumstances, typically, aren't nearly as stark. We tend to overexaggerate how stuck we are and how quicksand-like our lives have become. We act as if things just appear in our homes and our schedules are inevitable, rather than the result of our choices. This is not to diminish the impact of momentary situations outside of our control (e.g., taking care of a sick relative or a major work deadline). These are serious things, but they are the exceptions.

While the good news is that we can see how we have more choice in the matter than we realized, that may also be the tough news—we need to take greater responsibility for our circumstances and our emotional reactions to those circumstances. With this understanding, we can see that there is always a choice.

The right/wrong false dichotomy

One of the surprising discoveries I've made in my business (and when talking to people generally) is that people treat choices and big decisions as if there are right and wrong answers. Or good and bad choices only. It's not that these dichotomies are never present; it's that they present themselves far less frequently than is commonly assumed.

This dichotomy offers damaging black-and-white thinking. Maybe one choice would be best short-term but not long-term. Maybe another choice won't produce the result you were seeking, but it allows for another unexpected and positive outcome. The decisions we make aren't siloed in our lives. They interact with all our other decisions, making the dichotomy a narrow and ineffective mental infrastructure.

We rarely have the information we need to make "the best" decision. There is no way to know the future, so we can't make fully informed decisions about anything with future-dependent factors. We assume we can think ten steps ahead or that we are more knowledgeable about the application of statistics and risk management than we are.

You put too much pressure on yourself to win a no-win scenario. Take off the stress to get it right, especially as your answers may change over time or given new information. In other words, these dichotomies can drive us crazy for no good reason.

Trade-offs

When we see everything as a choice, it's empowering. On the flip side, it emphasizes the decision-making struggles we're already overwhelmed by or that we spend too much time on. A pivotal mindset shift is to look at most of our choices as trade-off events, however minor at times. Let's first get on the same page about the definition of trade-off: It's a balance achieved between two desirable but incompatible features, like a compromise. Some may shirk at the idea of compromise as it can be perceived as "less than" or giving in to something you don't really want.

I suggest a more positive perspective. A trade-off is when you acknowledge that you want something, like something, and/ or enjoy something, but put it aside in deference to something better. Or when you say yes to something, knowing it means you're implicitly saying no to something else. You want to buy a new whittling knife, but you also want a new portable speaker. You can't afford both, so you purchase the one you want more or would find more useful. Or you have two sun hats, though you're rarely out in the sun, so you only need one. You'll come across more of these trade-offs between two discrete items. Though it's not always as clear-cut.

Let's say you want that whittling knife but you're also saving up for a new car. You don't buy the knife so you can get closer to your goal of purchasing the new car. (So that you can go to more whittling conventions!) The connection between these two items is clearly related to saving money.

Then, things can become more complex. You may consider a trade-off between a whole group of things to get something else. In this complex mixture, time, money, mental and emotional energy, and the benefits of minimalism are weighed. Perhaps you have a couple of different video game consoles and dozens of games for each. You want to downsize what you have, but it would involve the time to research which console would be best to sell, go through the process, select which games to keep, etc. A lot of time would be spent on this effort, and you'd still be playing video games that take up five to ten hours a week.

Instead, you decide to make a trade-off: You get rid of every-thing wholesale, dropping it all off at a nearby gaming store (even though you won't make as much of a profit), give the media cabinet you stored it all in to a friend, and stop playing altogether to get some of your time back to spend on exercise. Now you have more room for your new exercise equipment. Video games and exercising aren't directly related, but they can be addressed in a trade-off together. Trading the time you could have spent researching and selling for the best price for a lower sale price and letting go of all video game-related decisions in one fell swoop. Independent of anything else, you may have made piecemeal or incremental decisions about gaming but now see how decisions can impact each other.

On a one-by-one basis, we can't see how an extra backup printer or third pair of sneakers makes a difference when downsizing. Same with items we may use on occasion but simply aren't as important as other things in our lives. It's an accumulation of all these things that get entered into the trade-off computation, which, in essence, is the decision to pursue minimalism. A minimalist lifestyle is what you're trading for, so keep that in mind when making small, "one-off" decisions that don't seem impactful independently but will make a difference when considered together. In other words, don't miss the forest for the trees. Each individual item you want to keep may seem worth keeping when not compared to "the forest" of your new lifestyle.

It's another reason to be clear on your goals and priorities. Within the context of our own lives, these siloed decisions may make sense, but when you view through a wider lens to see the effects on your finances and daily stressors, multiple rationalized decisions have a greater effect. It's truly "a whole is greater than the sum of its parts" type of scenario. In this case, the greater is typically not great in the scheme of what would improve your life.

With greater awareness about the importance of decision-making, I encourage you to learn and practice this skill. While there are many resources you can turn to, a book such as Annie Duke's *How to Decide* is a good start. She is a famous poker player, after all. Also, think about how you view choices and your ability to make them. Then, in Part 6 Put It into Practice, I'll show you how to reduce decision-making during the downsizing process and then how to streamline life systems to cut down on daily choices.

EXERCISES
Practice of Poverty and Fear Setting

Fears about the future drive decisions that are often not in your best interest. Giving less credence to those fears will help you make better downsizing choices. However, figuring out how to loosen the grip of those fears can be tough and is a substantial component of creating a minimalist mindset. We can utilize some mental exercises born from Stoicism to help us address this challenge.

When you hear the word *Stoic*, you may imagine the emotionless, grim look of a person, unmoved. But Stoicism is an ancient Greek philosophy gaining renewed interest as we search for practical life frameworks and tools. Stoicism is a way of life based on the premise of self-control, fortitude, and emotional resilience as the means to a good life. Specifically, it focuses on the distinction between what we can control and what we cannot. External events we cannot control teach us that we still have control through our choices about how we respond. This makes us less impulsive (e.g., the impulse to buy something). Not only are some aspects of this mindset in line with Meaningful Minimalism, but it also offers us two exercises we can use to further our mindset change.

The Practice of Poverty

Seneca, one of the great teachers of Stoicism, suggested the Practice of Poverty as a way of training oneself to release anxieties about what it would be like to lose it all. There is so much grasping and holding on in this material world of ours. If we can practice what it's like to have little, it can help us let go of some of that fear, seeing for ourselves that we would likely be okay. The Practice of Poverty exercise reframes the rest of what we own and have access to as fortunate extras we can appreciate more. It also may highlight which extras are most important to us.

This exercise has us look at what we wear, what we eat, and all our material conveniences. In modern practice, this may look like eating inexpensive, plain foods with the sole objective of sustaining energy and not wearing makeup or dressing up with jewelry or nice clothing. A week is commonly suggested to experience the Practice of Poverty fully. If you don't commit to a full week, mentally immersing yourself in the idea and possibly trying it out for a day or two would still be beneficial. Perhaps you've camped or lived on a shoestring budget as you entered adulthood. You can pull from these experiences as well and consider how you felt at the time and how you made it work.

Fear Setting

The Fear Setting exercise, unlike the previous one, which could result in you eating beans and rice for a week, is more theoretical. It was developed by *The Four-Hour Workweek* author Tim Ferriss, and it's based on the Stoics' "premeditation of evils," which has you conjure up the worst that can happen in a given situation and sit with it. Imagine it's really happening. Remove the barrier between the idea and the reality of what life would be like if it came to pass. With that reality in mind, you can complete Ferriss's Fear Setting exercise. Write a description of this scenario. Then ask yourself three questions: What are you afraid will be taken away from you? What can go wrong? What solutions can you implement? Next, take this scenario through time. What happens next?

It's effective because it forces us to detail the very fears that prevent us from taking difficult but necessary steps toward a minimalist lifestyle. In articulating them, you acknowledge them. You may realize that they aren't nearly as bad as you thought. Other times, well, they are. But sitting with them lessens the impulse to turn away, and then you could figure out what you would do if the fear came true. You realize that life would move on, you'd figure out a reasonable plan, and you'd be okay.

For example, we can plan how to best initiate a conversation with our partner about downsizing our home even though, in the past, it's resulted in a fight. We can plan ahead what we want to say and at what point(s) to pause the conversation if it gets heated. And then determine the point at which a couples' counselor could be considered to assist in navigating the challenge. A plan builds confidence in our resiliency, and we realize our fears are far scarier than reality. We can handle our fears coming true (which may not even happen!) and that everything will be okay.

Our fears of letting go are emotional drivers that seem too big to battle when staring down at an attic or stepping back into an old storage unit. If, instead, we ask how bad it would really be if we let go of stuff that has been sitting on the chopping block for years, we may realize that our fears are just fears and not reasons to hold on. We don't want to live in a home filled with fear-based possessions. That's not going to feel good. When fear is released, barriers come down. Then, we can rebuild our mindset to one less predicated on what scares us and more on how we can proactively build the life we want.

EXERCISE
Perspective-Shifting Visualization

While we've gotten granular in the process of rebuilding, it's necessary to take an enormous leap back. Give yourself some time and space with a much broader view. Shift your perspective. The process of letting go and sifting through years of minutiae in the form of unorganized paperwork, your button collection, and a second set of utensils is a black hole. That doesn't mean none of it matters. It means you need a break. This is common, and you can get yourself out of it.

The visualization technique I suggest starts with the image of infinite stars. Imagine: You are but a speck of dust in the universe. A speck of dust on one of the estimated one hundred billion planets in our galaxy, which is one of two trillion galaxies in the observable universe (and who knows how many universes!). Allow yourself to drift toward the magnitude of the solar system; watch the moons circle their planets and then planets circle around the sun. Imagine our planet as if you were on a space shuttle, and notice its patches of blue. If that universal scale is too difficult to reach in your mind's eye, think about majestic nature scenes: mountain ranges, endless fields, a flock of birds, fluffy clouds, a calm lake. Consider billions of people of different cultures spread across the globe today. Life is no longer small. It is incalculable. That massiveness and expanse make life feel less heavy and almost simple.

Everything is perspective, and if you relate the fleeting nature of life and our mathematical insignificance to the massive emotions and self-importance we carry, the differential comes into focus.

You are but a speck of dust. Rebuild from that humble insight.

The Value of Change

Letting go of our stuff is hard, but so are long-held beliefs and ways of thinking. While mindset change is the quickest and most lasting path to minimalism, change is hard, period. It also takes time. You have to work on it with intention. Completing this part of the book is only the beginning of mindset change. Remember, this is an iterative process.

I suggest rereading the Vow to Be Honest chapter to let it sink in more fully and to ensure you build a minimalist mindset that's true to you. Continue clarifying your values and priorities and educate yourself about relevant topics.

Then, you will start to see your life and the world differently. As your mindset changes, decision-making will require less effort, and your intuition will sharpen. The process of creating and maintaining a minimalist life will be quicker and truer to your desires.

Part V

But Wait!

We're about ready to put the results of your internal exploration into practice. You have clarity on why you're about to downsize and organize and a steady frame of mind about it. Maybe you're so excited that you've already begun getting rid of things and are sure nothing will stop you. Or this exploration has left you a bit overwhelmed, so you've developed a long list of reasons why you can't proceed with a minimalist lifestyle or will start working on it *later*.

The voices in our heads are very creative and pop in to encourage procrastination at various points during this process. It's those same voices that got you to this point in the first place, and they will cleverly develop more shields. Everything you've learned along the way has clarified and strengthened your resolve. But these voices and their excuses have had a lot of training. Part of mindset change and resilience is becoming a worthy contender.

Whether your excuses are already in hand or you develop them as we proceed, allow me to cut you off at the pass. I'll address the most common reasons for resistance and how to persist through them. We've already discussed this issue in various scenarios in previous sections to some extent, but here we will look at how to counteract all that resistance.

But I've Already Kondo'd!

"But I know where everything is!"

"But I have a system!"

"Having ten thousand emails in my inbox isn't a problem!"

"I've already Kondo'd!"

These assertions aren't in response to me telling someone that they have a problem. It's after they come to me because they do, and then I suggest making a change or adopting a different system because the one they have isn't working. That's when the excuses begin. They're the type of excuse where you realize the sort of personal investment this will entail is significant and decide that, *actually*, you can manage just fine, as you've been doing, and, in fact, you've already gotten rid of a bunch of clothes or paperwork recently, so do you really need to bother?

If you've already invested effort and seen progress in downsizing, learning that you're only a quarter of the way there, that your systems are far from efficient, or that taking things to the next level will require the heavy labor we've been avoiding may leave you wanting to sweep things under the rug (or lots of rugs).

Sometimes, I discuss a specific category of items with a client like coats and jackets. I might suggest letting go of some of them due to lack of use and duplication. They resist because they went through them when they read, you guessed it, *The Life-Changing Magic of Tidying Up* by Marie Kondo. They may have let go of half their coats and jackets then. That's when I remind them that the fact that they were able to let go of some stuff is proof of how capable they are of letting go and continuing this process. We're looking for the best possible end state. How much they previously said goodbye to has no bearing on what that end state is. We often dig deeper and talk through each item more, and the pile quickly becomes smaller.

Many homes I've organized had at least one, if not a handful, of minimalism or organizing books on overstuffed bookshelves (or in floor piles). We may exchange a few jokes about the irony as we come across them, but despite the progress they made before I entered the scene, there's significantly more to do as they still struggle to find their passport or sunglasses or recent tax documents. Things that spark joy in the moment only mean so much when you never know where your keys are.

Whatever work you've accomplished based on a blog or a book (or professional organizer) involved steps in the right direction. But you wouldn't be reading this book if you've already addressed many of the lifestyle changes that Meaningful Minimalism can offer. If you're managing for now, that means your house is essentially filled with band-aids. You know that it can't last, and why in the world do you just want to *manage* instead of *thrive*?

But I Don't Want to Hurt People's Feelings!

Did you read the Vow to Be Honest chapter? Answer honestly. While it brings truthfulness to the forefront of our thinking, honesty may feel extra uncomfortable when beginning to take action or thinking about taking actions that *may* make others feel bad. Meaning that we're making it about us just as much as we're concerned about others' experiences. We desire not to feel the negative sensation associated with hurting someone's feelings—though we often have preconceived notions and projections about how other people feel and will react. It's not your job to manage someone else's emotions. Typically, we stress ourselves out in the attempt and may get it wrong anyway.

Our own guilt or shame tends to tie in directly with not wanting to hurt others' feelings, as cultural and societal expectations are no joke. They are powerful but potentially detrimental if not considered carefully. They shouldn't completely hijack our choices. Instead, we'll consider trade-offs based on personal values and goals versus what feels easiest in the moment.

For example, keeping hand-me-downs may feel like a kindness to those who "gifted" us the items. But looking deeper, this kindness may be a mask for the undefinable guilt of relinquishing family possessions. You think you're doing something wrong. You're not. You're caught in family dynamics and the trickiness that the responsibility of ownership entails.

If you're avoiding minimalism-related choices because you fear hurting someone, first investigate whether that fear is based in reality, and if it is, *how true* it is. It may only be a mild concern for them, if at all. This is the case more often than we think. When I told my family that I no longer wanted to participate in our family's holiday gift exchange, I explained it from the standpoint of my personal values and how it would help us all be less stressed and save money. They weren't particularly happy about it or even fully on board. But they weren't angry. They understood that I wasn't asking for less family time; we would still get together—just without gifts. It was also my choice not to give or receive gifts; they could still do what they wanted otherwise. It was an uncomfortable but honest and respectful conversation. It took a few years, but they eventually adopted my approach and have even thanked me for it. Change can be awkward at first, but if I'd kept quiet because I didn't want to hurt anyone's feelings, we wouldn't have evolved in a positive direction.

If the minimalism-related choice you're considering really will hurt someone's feelings, and you don't want to risk upsetting them, scheme different ways to reach the desired endpoint. Maybe it's scripting how you want to broach the subject, enlisting the help of someone else, or maybe telling 80 percent of the truth to start.

If you are willing to risk upsetting them, even with a tactful approach (which you should always use because kindness is still important), you can accept that someone's sensitivity isn't your responsibility. Listen to them express their discontent, respond clearly to their concerns, and make them feel heard while keeping your ground.

Occasionally, not rocking the boat in a relationship can make it worth keeping the trinket your mother-in-law gave you on the mantel. This is a great example of a trade-off we may make from time to time. Everything does not need to become a principled stance. But recognize that you're making a conscious choice with kindness and honesty.

But I Want to Be the Hero!

Keeping things in order to be "the hero" happens when we want to be prepared for any scenario for the sake of other people. We want to show our value but, as a result, may be keeping stuff for ourselves or others that isn't necessary. The reality is that we don't need to keep our homes filled with stuff just for these one-off and seldom-realized situations.

Catering to our family and friends and helping them feel at home is a part of building enriching relationships. However, sometimes well-meaning intentions become excuses for keeping too much stuff. For instance, wanting to be prepared for every possible guest request: extra pillows and towels, tons of little toiletries, etc. Sometimes, this happens the other way around, and we don't want to throw something away, like a box of tea we'll never drink. We use the excuse of a guest potentially wanting some as a reason to keep it. In other words, we've used the "hero" excuse as a way to rationalize keeping something.

Don't we all know the "cord guy" who slings in every length of HDMI cable or iPhone charging cable? I've had many similar clients who get excited by having the perfect thing for someone in need at the perfect time. This makes them feel useful, smart, and valuable (and serves as reinforcement for their pack rat tendencies). My client Matt had an extensive bungee cord collection (among other collections) from which he happily let neighbors borrow. I saw this value and suggested keeping a collection still but reducing it significantly.

The next time we met, he said that his neighbor had just asked to borrow a bungee cord, and the perfect length would have been ten inches. After the reduction, he only had a six-inch and a twelve-inch. This was his "proof" that he should have kept them all. But this was not proof of anything. The twelve-inch, while not perfect, did the job his neighbor needed, and quite frankly, if he had no bungee cords to lend, his neighbor would have easily come up with an alternate solution. We make things a much bigger deal than they are to justify keeping stuff.

If you multiply that by the number of other such collections and don't want to spend all that much time on organizing, it's not a worthwhile trade-off to have a house overrun with stuff for the off-chance someone might need something you have. Having the right thing at the right time for someone may hurt more than it helps because to replicate this good feeling and identify with the hero role, you keep unnecessary items with expectations. This extra keeping and storage encourage materialism in some form and adds self-imposed responsibility in the form of organizing and storage, retrieval, and keeping track of what is loaned and to whom.

Sometimes, our desire to be the savior extends to a more specific role, like branding ourselves as the family historian. Within our families, it can feel meaningful and satisfying to keep family photos and other heirlooms or essentially become the family's genealogist. We might feel a sense of responsibility about this or attach ourselves to the identity. However, being the family historian may not be appreciated by our family. We might be spinning our wheels and wasting our time with something no one really cares about but we've convinced ourselves they do. Or we wish they did.

When these hero-driven choices become frequent and impassioned enough, they become part of our identity. When we identify with these types of actions, they take on a meaning of their own, and they prevent us from making the best decisions, as we discussed in Part 2: Let Go of Your Identity. Take time to consider what things you're keeping for hero or family historian purposes. Resist the temptation to keep stuff for the sole purpose of being the hero. Re-evaluate where this makes sense and is meaningful to everyone involved. Be specific and intentional so that this *but* doesn't interrupt your downsizing flow.

But My Parents Don't Mind My Stuff!

"I'll just leave my stuff there until they move."

"I don't have the house I've always dreamed of yet, so I need to keep my things there until I do."

"I told my parents they can just go through and get rid of the stuff in my old room."

"I don't want to have this conversation with my parents. It's too stressful."

"I can't afford to move this stuff to a storage unit. Shouldn't I be *saving* money?"

I've heard these proclamations a hundred times over. They are common *later* excuses that create more problems than they solve. Do you still have stuff at your parents' house? (Or are you a parent who keeps stuff for their kids?) Maybe it's time to rethink that strategy.

Whether you're eighteen or forty-eight, your parents' home can be a seemingly safe repository for the stuff you wish to keep but allow to be out of sight, out of mind. After you initially leave, some of your possessions remain at home as an innocent default. You move out of state and can't bring everything at once, aren't sure whether you'll be moving back, or simply don't have the room in your new digs. This rite of passage is seldom traversed if there isn't another impetus for change.

In your mind, there will be a time when you have a bigger home or feel more settled. So many established adults see their homes as transient, even if they own a small house or are married. You don't know how or if your preferences will change. You may think your parents want to keep your stuff because they miss you or that they don't mind being your storage unit. What you don't know is that they may secretly be counting the days until you finally pick it all up or they can throw it all away. Perhaps they hold an attachment to it as a way of holding back time, wanting to feel a connection to your childhood. Maybe it's simply a mild irritation.

You may be storing a few curated items that you know you want to save but don't need regular access to like photo albums. There may be mystery boxes awaiting the moment you sift through their contents. There might be a bunch of childhood items scattered throughout your old room and other areas of their home that you visit on occasion. You never feel like going through your stuff while there, though you may discover an artifact of your youth, gushing, "Oh, I remember this!" It makes you feel really good (the fleeting glee trap). That good feeling is remembered and associated with a reunion with your stuff, so any thought of getting rid of such stuff is resisted because why would you give up an opportunity to feel good?

Postponing the inevitable necessity to address our temporarily stored stuff may feel okay at the moment. Finding a more sustainable solution could feel even better. Most importantly, this saves time and headaches for everyone in the long term.

Some questions to ask yourself are:

- If your parents threw out all your stuff without asking, would you be heartbroken, annoyed, or relieved?
- What is the point of keeping something for ten or twenty years that you may only use one day in the future?
- If it's a useful item, shouldn't someone else have the opportunity to experience its value instead of it being unused by anyone for several years (or, *gulp*, decades)?
- If it is a purely sentimental item, is it of paramount importance to retain it despite not cohabitating with it?

Parents downsizing their own homes may be the stimulus for change. Delaying the inevitable leaves you at the whim of your parents' timeline to go through such things finally, and this timing may not be convenient for you. It's best to get ahead of this situation. Then there is the much sadder transition, where one's parents pass away, and children must tend to the dismantling of a home and its memories. In such cases, these children tend to take on their parents' items as their own, reversing the cycle.

I had a client, the Andrews, who were referred to me by their daughter, Justine. They were recently retired, ready to downsize and sell their home of thirty-plus years, and move to a smaller place closer to Justine, her husband, and their new baby. One challenge during our work was that some of Justine's belongings were stored there, even though she helped hire me (and was forty years old). She was so tied up with her job and new baby that scheduling time with her to go through her stuff was very difficult!

Consider this: There are other things your parents can do with the space you've been occupying. Or you can become a good example for them; clearing out your possessions may prompt them to begin sorting through theirs. It may alert them to the fact that they have a much bigger home than they need. It will ensure that when they choose to downsize or move, there will be no time dependency with you to get your stuff or added stress for them.

It's tough to say goodbye to our safety nets, especially when they used to be our homes. You don't have to say goodbye completely: You can preserve carefully selected items in a memory box, take photos of items you don't plan to keep, or incorporate some items into your current home. Addressing the stuff we keep in our parents' homes is an easy way to help our parents while no longer holding onto the past.

But Other People Are the Problem!

While you've identified your downsizing and organizing challenges, you might find yourself diverting blame to your partner, children, parents, in-laws, friends, neighbors ... whomever. In doing so, you've articulated additional external (to you) challenges that must be addressed. Instead of using other people as an excuse not to get to work, we'll look at ways to solve these *other people* problems.

Let's start with couples. Whether new or long-time committed, partners have a bevy of things to disagree on, fight about, or be annoyed by. How much stuff they have, what the stuff is, how much money is spent on stuff, and how it's organized (or not) are commonly included in the cornucopia of complaints.

I'm usually hired by one person in a couple. One of two situations always occurs: (1) The partner who did not hire me has nothing to do with the project and is generally resistant to the idea; (2) both are engaged in the project, but each finds a moment to privately tell me how the other partner is actually the really disorganized one, and can I help get rid of their Beanie Baby collection?

I try to play this straight-faced. Mostly because I understand. There are reasons we keep the things we keep and why other things drive us mad. Some tend to keep things "just in case," while others love the latest gadgets. Some are minimalists. Others are maximalists. While we tend to differ in our preferences, priorities and values are important to respect. But as they relate to stuff, they can be just as divisive. Respecting your partner's perspective, which includes making an effort to understand it without judgment, is key.

Your partner is not patently wrong, messy, or disorganized. Everything is relative. Just because your shirts are tucked away in the back of the closet doesn't make you right and your partner, who leaves their old tee shirts scattered on the bedroom floor, wrong. We are all just different sides of the same coin. You might not enjoy their preferences. In fact, they may drive you crazy or tempt you to throw away their stuff when they're not looking. (Please don't do this!) Remember, that is your hang-up and a reminder that you haven't resolved your own issues yet. It's unfair to expect

196

your partner to meet your standards on your timeline. You may have unopened boxes with college papers or memorabilia your parents handed off to you.

It is always tricky to figure out how couples inhabit the same space, creating the nest they both want to live in. Problems related to stuff are magnified when we move past our own personal issues to deal with our partners'. This is an opportunity to become sensitive to their needs and challenges. Honesty, rather than lecturing or blaming, is necessary for a healthy home and relationship.

The place to start goes back to values and priorities. Revisit yours and seek to understand the others'. You may disagree at first but then make your way toward common ground. There may be areas where you agree to disagree or find compromises. As with most relationship issues, these are best addressed when not in the heat of the moment, when you are tripping over your partner's unfinished carpentry project, or can't find your favorite mug that you just left on the counter. Carve out some time to discuss the issue calmly.

We all come to relationships with baggage: our past loves, baked-in habits, financial concerns, and communication styles. Plus all the messy things that make up our personalities. We also come with literal bags of stuff and all our preferences (the stubborn ones and the silly ones). We need to be gentle with our partners and recognize that we aren't as different as we think. With time spent seeking to understand and calmly compromise, your partner can help you on this path toward less stuff rather than be another obstacle.

Expanding beyond romantic partnerships to roommates, friends, and other family members, we can't blame others for our situation. We are held back not because of other people but because of our limited ability to communicate with them. Developing a communication style to address minimalism-related issues not only prevents you from using other people as an excuse for inaction but can also help build closer relationships. While you shouldn't need a new communication approach specifically related to minimalism concerns, it may feel new to approach these topics (especially after reading this book).

Building upon communication strategies we've touched on so far, I recommend nonviolent communication. It's a compassionate form of communication created by Marshall Rosenberg in his seminal book, *Nonviolent Communication: A Language of Life*. It's based on the idea that we can express our feelings, based on our specific needs. It offers an opportunity to make a request for different behavior from your partner that is nonjudgmental and non-blaming. At the very least, consider developing prewritten scripts when you find it difficult to approach these topics … or give them a copy of this book.

Minimalism is an opportunity to strengthen relationships because it asks us to be intentional. You can't use other people as an excuse when you always have a choice. Honesty and better communication will help you overcome this type of resistance. Work *with* people, not against them.

But I'm a Creative Person!

While I've encouraged you to be careful about attaching to your identities, I encourage you to (loosely) maintain the identity of a creative person. Further, I encourage everyone who doesn't see themselves as creative to open their mind to this moniker.

Sometimes, I worry that I'm sending the wrong message and that people find these ideas about minimalism and organizing lacking room for fun, creativity, and spontaneity. Or perhaps that these ideas are too restraining. I think it's the opposite. Minimalism doesn't limit creativity; it helps strengthen your creative muscles.

Once each item is organized, and surfaces are cleared, we might find ourselves in the uncomfortable position of not wanting to disrupt this delicate balance. We might fear that spreading out creative projects on the kitchen table would ruin this immaculate space. Instead, think of minimalism as creating a space for mess. This can be for a few hours, a few days, or maybe a few weeks. Life can be messy, and that's not a bad thing. Here, you can enjoy it.

Another benefit of adopting a more minimalist lifestyle is to give yourself unencumbered room to just live. Space is where we can create, experience peace, and use our imaginations. In this space, we have the perfect spot for letting life happen organically and without constrictions. Not a space that mingles with other messes, gets subsumed by them, or becomes permanent, but rather a temporary space to play.

Consider how the space you opened up in your home can be used. Let your creativity loose.

The point of having this newfound space in your home is to actually enjoy your home and feel like you have room to breathe. Space to breathe also brings us away from distractions that might derail our creative projects. You don't need a bigger house for this type of space. You can create it by doing away with the stuff in your life that distracts, doesn't bring you meaning, and that you can simply do without.

Along the lines of creativity, we have varying degrees of self-expression that shine through what we display in our homes and how we adorn ourselves. When you begin to analyze the design of your home (or lack thereof) and the shoes you've collected, you may feel resistant to letting them go because you view them as forms of self-expression. They are how you differentiate yourself from others, how you express a mood or point of view, and how you express creativity. Those motivations are pure and understandable. The skill is to find the most minimalist way to be self-expressive and be discerning when deciding what stays for this reason.

The need to express who you are through these means also expresses who you are in other ways. For example, if you chose to use ozone-depleting hairspray to construct your self-expressing hairstyle, that would be you saying that you value your chosen hairstyle rather than the environmental consequences of hairspray usage. While how you do your hair is self-expression here, it's multifold.

If you're careful about what you choose to keep in your home and what to wear, you can still vividly express yourself. You would not be relinquishing the ability to make design choices, but the palette from which to choose will be inherently more limited. Which is a good thing. Not only because it will be simpler and quicker to get yourself ready in the morning, but with limitations, we become adept at refining. We have more opportunities for creativity. If your wardrobe is unlimited, you just pick something off the shelf and throw it on because it tickled your fancy at the store. With a more limited wardrobe, you find ways to make your wardrobe mix and match more effectively and use more of what you have because it's more accessible and intentional.

The same is true of your home. Why not decorate with fresh flowers and branches that you pluck from nature and put in repurposed glass vases? The pieces of nature would represent where you have been and what colors or textures pulled at you. You could also change these often, which would allow you to change your personal space more often. Maybe you're the opposite and haven't found your style or creative footing. Minimalism can help here as you look at your *whys*, goals, and priorities and adopt a new mindset to focus on what matters most to you.

Being a creative person isn't an excuse for not moving forward with minimalism, as being creative means you have a desirable talent to devise minimalist solutions. You'll also enjoy the removal of distractions and the added space for creativity to bloom. Remember that you can have all the creative supplies that you need—just remember to be honest with yourself about whether you're using them.

But I Don't Want It to Go to the Landfill!

My client Corrine was ruminating endlessly about something she wanted to get rid of but didn't know how.

Three old bottles of half-used nail polish.

"I can't find anyone who wants them, and I don't want to use beauty products that have chemicals in them. But there must be a way to dispose of them sustainably, right?"

Her intentions were clear and in line with her values. She was frustrated that there wasn't a responsible way to address the consequences of a few old, unfinished bottles of nail polish no longer being needed. At the time she purchased the nail polish, she didn't know as much about sustainability or the health concerns surrounding certain products. We relive Corinne's conundrum ad nauseam when "trying to do the right thing."

More searching for a taker could have been done. Or there may have been some avenue for reuse that I hadn't discovered. But at a certain point, the effort wasn't worth the three half-empty bottles. But she resisted the idea of throwing them into the trash. By delaying the inevitable, she could avoid the guilty feeling associated with tossing them. Her reaction is not uncommon.

This scenario is an example of an issue that I call *landfill purgatory*. It's when you start turning your home into a makeshift landfill intermediary by delaying the inevitable, typically out of guilt. Sometimes, it's also because of the sunk cost fallacy or overvaluing what you own (endowment effect), even though it's no longer helpful, reusable, or recyclable. No one wants anything to go into the landfill. There are only different levels of remorse. and expectations of landfill-alternative options when letting go of an item.

Identifying disposal options like giving items to friends, donating, reusing, and recycling are all sustainability-positive moves and part of the experience of letting go. But there is another side: You have things that you don't need either because you bought them before your values, knowledge, or tastes changed or you accepted them without thinking. While it's important to reflect upon where your stuff goes next, it's more important to prevent it from coming into your possession in the first place. The more significant hurdle is not to stop holding on; it's to not grab hold. The focus is on the wrong side of the equation. Don't wait to see the problem until after the fact.

Until you integrate prevention and "begin with the end in mind" thinking (we'll discuss more in Part 7: Continuous Care), we have to address things as they are and not get off track from your purging process. Keeping items in your home that you no longer need creates a *landfill purgatory* and delays the inevitable. You aren't avoiding the landfill, only when it gets there. Putting those destined-for-the-landfill items in the trash (if there aren't viable alternatives) is an important part of this process. It's part of coming face to face with the consequences of our actions.

Giving something to a friend or donating it doesn't mean it won't go to the landfill, either. You may be convinced your friend wants something, but they were actually just being polite (as you have been). Or maybe they thought they wanted it at first, but a couple of months later it's in the trash bin, and you are left with a false sense of landfill diversion. Donation centers don't resell everything they receive for various reasons. In other words, people want your stuff less than you think and may not be as considerate about their disposal as you would be.

This doesn't mean you shouldn't recycle, reuse, donate, or give stuff to friends. Anything you can do to avoid the landfill and get more use out of a product is ideal. You can avoid *landfill purgatory* in the future by recognizing that so much of your stuff will take up residence in the landfill in the end, despite your best intentions. It's better for you to make more informed purchases and collect as little as possible.

Don't use avoidance of the landfill as an excuse for inaction. To avoid falling into the *landfill purgatory* trap, take the uncomfortable moment now. Think about what led you to drop items in the trash so you can more deeply understand why you want to prevent those moments in the future. Corinne did. By throwing away those bottles of nail polish, she relinquished guilt, avoided *landfill purgatory*, and learned a lesson that she will carry with her in all her future purchases.

But I've Worked Hard! I
Deserve My Things!

Regardless of how hard you've worked, how many degrees you have, how much money you earn, or what the media and advertisements claim, I'm sorry, but you don't deserve anything. I'm sure you're wonderful, and I want you to have a happy and fulfilling life. However, as we discussed in the Systems and Imagined Realities chapter, the concept of deserving does little to help us, doesn't reflect reality, and can lead to a sense of entitlement.

If you have any shot at simplifying your life, the excuse that you deserve a new set of golf clubs, another purse, or whatever the Instagram ads told you to buy during your last scroll has to go out along with your trash and recycling bags. Even when it comes to experiences, you don't deserve a vacation or a spa visit. Regardless of the type of purchase, we're not entitled to this stuff.

This sense of entitlement is different from the *shoulds* we discussed at the beginning of the book, which steer us toward decisions that don't align with who we are and what we want. However, entitlement similarly leads to the idea that we have a right to certain things. Wanting to improve your life and earn money is perfectly fine and not at odds with minimalism. In fact, minimalism makes more room for intentional ambition. However, to create a minimalist lifestyle based on what's most meaningful, ensuring that what you do or buy will truly better your life takes discernment. You'll get off track if it comes from entitlement at the root.

We don't have a universal right to buy and accumulate whatever we want. When you work hard, when you are busy or stressed, or even *just because*, look out for the trap of rationalizing that you deserve a new dress, new gadget, or new car. When you work hard or have been through hardship, that is a part of life. You don't then become entitled to things to compensate.

If you find yourself resisting this downsizing work when you sort through specific items you believe you deserve or you resist this process as a whole because you believe you deserve more material goods and don't want to think about the consequences of your accumulation, double-check whether this sense of entitlement is helping or hurting you.

But I'll Miss My Stuff!

When you experience the feeling of missing something, do you assume that something went wrong, a mistake was made, or things should be different? The fear of missing keeps us from letting go of something, particularly with personal or sentimental items. It keeps us so fixated on the possibility of regret that we miss an opportunity to let go. We miss a chance to move toward simplicity because we'll go to great lengths to avoid the experience of missing.

I recall chatting with my mom after my parents downsized from my childhood suburban home to a two-bedroom condo in a retirement community. She parted with countless decades of things in the downsizing process. Knowing that many of her memories were wrapped in the material world, I asked whether she missed anything that she let go of. I was surprised when she said, "Not much." She explained that sometimes she'd reach for a specific vase and realize that she no longer had it. "Then, what would happen?" I asked. Apparently, nothing, really. She'd momentarily remember how beautiful it was, grab a different vase, and continue with her day.

I know she experienced stress in deciding which vases to give away. We magnify and intensify how the moment of missing will be experienced. When you think, "Maybe I should have kept that," or "I wish I still had that," it's a fleeting moment in reality. But in the drama of our imaginations, it's a deterrent to making choices that will improve our lives overall. When we latch on to the fear of potential regret and the over-weighing of what that moment of regret will mean, we lose track of what's most important. It's hard to appreciate missing if you think it'll be all bad.

We forget that missing means you cared or maybe even that you loved. Missing starts with something beautiful.

My mom's stories about the people in our family who have passed primarily reside in her memories and the stories she tells. But like some, she finds part of her connection to the past through family heirlooms. But these heirlooms aren't hidden. She keeps them on display and uses them. She tells their stories when in use to bring memories to life. She leans into the beauty of missing people she cared about but isn't just holding on to these items because of fear of guilt or doing the wrong thing for historical purposes.

But more often than not, fear of missing takes the form of unused items packed away in unmarked boxes in an attic, basement, or closet corner. We lose something by keeping all the room and mental space we'd have if we were open to letting go—a lighter life. Instead of acknowledging the beauty of missing, we're stuck in the fear trap.

Missing can happen in a brief moment when we remember having an object we used to use (like my mom's vase), or it may elongate into a state of being. Even with people, there's a sadness to the happiness and vice versa: You have someone wonderful to miss. Missing conjures up love just as much as it signifies the longing. We focus so much on the past that we ignore the present state. Either way, we need to unpack what the missing means. And acknowledge that it might not mean much.

Perhaps you push yourself to let go of so much that you end up missing something to the extent that you realize it would have been better to keep it. If you miss it enough, it might shape future decisions on what to accumulate and keep. Missing something that you would have preferred to keep teaches you more about what types of things are okay to miss and highlights any areas where you may want to be more careful about what you let go of in the future. There are no mistakes; only lessons.

The fear of missing things distracts us from strategic downsizing. Missing will no longer be seen as a mistake that you have to go to great lengths to sidestep. Instead, it can be an emotion weaved through the fabric of your multi-dimensional life. It can add a particular type of richness. And it can remind you of your strength in letting things go.

No *Buts*

We're all excuse-making machines, whether those excuses are built upon a lack of honesty with ourselves or come from the discomfort of completing this project's challenging tasks (for example, saying the hard things to ourselves and others). We make excuses as an act of avoidance, as some of this work is simply annoying and dull! And yes, sometimes we make excuses out of pure laziness.

While the previous excuses are not an exhaustive list, I encourage you to keep track of any areas of aversion. While you can't fully combat all these excuses before beginning the downsizing and organizing process, become aware of the ones you've identified and be on the lookout for them once you begin.

Occasionally, they can be clues or warning signs of bigger issues or problems not directly related to creating a minimalist lifestyle. Don't ignore them completely but rather learn to listen to them with scrutiny. After a while, the excuses we conjure up can seem almost funny. Don't forget to see the humor in this process and try to keep it light when you can.

Part VI

Put It into Practice

This is when you realize you've read most of this book and have done a lot of thinking and emotional investigating … and not a single item in your home has left the nest. (Though perhaps you felt inspired while reading and got started. If so, congratulations!)

Your minimalism pre-work has prepared you to put your new mindset into practice. We'll integrate it to flesh out your goals, priorities, and vision for your new minimalist lifestyle. I'll walk you through creating a project plan and propose a strategy for implementation. I'll provide solutions to common challenges and strategies to make all of this not feel like such a downer. While I can't apply all my organizing techniques to your unique situation from these pages, I'll set you up for the work and teach you some of its principles. Finally, we'll address the stuff that isn't stuff at all—lifestyle areas.

Define Your Goals, Priorities, and Vision

Before you start, you'll have to clarify three pillars of your own minimalist lifestyle: your goals, priorities, and vision. Don't worry—all the work we've done so far makes up the building blocks needed to bring you to clarity. Reflect back on your *why*, your values, your more general goals, what's meaningful to you, and how you've defined your problems. This is all important fodder for the following:

Goals and objectives

We touched on lifestyle alignment with goals in Part 1: Define Your *Why* to generally explore whether alignment was a *why* itself and to start investigating your life goals. While you can have specific goals related to the downsizing and organizing work itself, like canceling a storage unit, feeling more confident when you have company, and organizing your kitchen, we want to be sure those organizing goals relate to your grander, non-organizing-related goals and the bigger picture of your lifestyle as a whole.

Next up, I'm going to ask you to get clear on your goals and objectives. You may have already started this work with the exercises in Part 1. If so, use that work as a foundation to finesse this list. Reminder: A *goal* is a state that you want to arrive at (long term or short term), in service of moving toward your North Star, or your intention—which likely mirrors the *why* you previously discovered. An *objective* is a specific achievement to help you reach your goal. (The process to accomplish those objectives is composed of specific tasks, but we're not there yet, so for the moment, focus on your goals and objectives.)

All that said, don't get too tripped up by the terminology. As long as you're working from a hierarchical vantage point, from broader lifestyle aspirations to more specific steps required to achieve those aspirations, you'll get to where you need to go. We want to start broad so we're going in the right direction and then get granular so it becomes actionable.

For example, if your intentions are to slow down in life and prepare for an early retirement, your list may look like this:

Goal 1: Slow Down (short-term)
Objective 1: Only engage in hobbies and relationships that are most important to me

This may involve letting go of certain hobbies and the objects that I have in order to do such a hobby.

Objective 2: To be more efficient with my time

This may involve improving my tasks and calendar system.

Both objectives support my ability to slow down by freeing up more time. Maybe to slow down I need other support like creating a mindful morning ritual. I can add that as a goal too.

Goal 2: Prepare for early retirement (long-term)
Objective 1: Have a downsized home

This may involve selling items, letting go of storage units, and living in a less expensive home, all of which will save money to be put toward retirement and added to savings on a monthly basis. Any of these would be broader tasks to reach this goal.

Objective 2: Have a clear financial plan and systems

This may involve downsizing and organizing all my paper and digital files, making tough decisions about spending habits, and creating a financial maintenance plan.

Your turn: Look at the lists you made in Part 1 and break them down into goals and objectives that are aligned with your *why*. You don't need to be comprehensive. In fact, please don't. It will be overwhelming, which is the opposite of what we intend. Remember too that these goals shouldn't be directly about minimalism, but about the outcomes you want to achieve for a simplified lifestyle.

Priorities

Setting goals is a lot of fun, and it's easy to get carried away with long lists of things you're eager to achieve. But, unfortunately, none of us has the time, money, or energy to do everything at once. That's where priorities come in. These are the concerns, interests, and desires that stand out above the rest of the stuff you have going on in your life—the top priorities are simply the things that are more important than others. They are what you value and pay attention to.

So, go back to that goals list and review it with your top priorities in mind. Which two or three are most important to you at this moment in your life?

Remember, your goals and priorities are not specific to minimalism—they're related to your larger life aspirations. The point is for all your minimalism-related planning and implementation *to be in service to your priorities*. You may find that some of your priorities only call for a couple of small minimalism-related tasks, while others require large-scale minimalism work to achieve.

Your priority list might be:

1. Advance my career.
2. Spend more time with my family.
3. Build confidence in my ability to be productive and on top of things.

See some overlap? Streamlining and organizing possessions as you downsize will help build confidence in productivity, and all that productivity confidence is a skill to help advance one's career.

So, although "advance career" doesn't seem like a minimalism-specific priority, it's all related. Your Meaningful Minimalism efforts will be designed to support career advancement and your other priorities by influencing how you spend your time, money, and mental and emotional bandwidth. If you remove the time and financial cost of, let's say, learning to play the tuba because it's not a priority, you can take the time and money you'd previously spent on that to take a course that will buoy your career. Articulating your priorities highlights how you should be spending your time and money.

Before reading this book, you may not have realized you're not currently living your priorities. Understanding why this misalignment happened in the first place can be helpful as you correct it. To that end, it may be useful to track your time over a week to see how much is spent in service to your priorities and how much is spent on less important (or even distracting) endeavors. Maybe you realize that something you didn't list as a priority really is one for you, or something you thought was a priority either isn't actually one or isn't getting the treatment it deserves.

With your intentions, goals, and priorities defined, you're ready to develop your vision for your improved life! This vision—a clear idea of how you want your home and lifestyle to look—is one of the strongest motivators available. But as I'll keep reminding you, this is an iterative process, so nothing is set in stone. Be clear on these items, but don't let a desire for perfection keep you from making progress. You can always go back and refine further.

Creating a Meaningful Minimalism vision

Visualizing is a way to clarify goals such that you can begin to see them applied in your life—sort of like practical daydreaming. It's time to take out the proverbial blank sheet of paper and outline a vision of what you *want* your life to be. Caution: Don't let yourself get bogged down with the details of where you are now. We tend to begin where we are and try to conceive of cutting back or rearranging. That's a limiting approach. We need to see the big picture before we can take a deep dive into the minutiae of our stuff. How will you know how many bookshelves you need to keep if you haven't seen whether any of them even belong in your new home vision?

Right now, I want you to start with nothing, visualize what you want, and *then* determine what you need.

Creating a generalized blueprint helps to motivate and guide us. Regardless of where you draw inspiration and ideas, be sure your visualization is entirely your own. Otherwise, you'll be chasing someone else's ideal and get off track. Plus, your functional needs can't be articulated through someone else's design alone.

Here's an example. My client Jasmine was moving from a three-bedroom, three-level rowhouse filled with old memories, furniture, and a little bit of mayhem to a nine-hundred-square-foot, two-bedroom apartment in a different state.

Our first session involved visualizing her new place. We didn't start with anything she had in her current space; rather, we imagined the layout of her new space, completely empty. Then we discussed uses and functionality: what the second bedroom would be used for, what her office needs were, where she would watch TV, whether there would be a formal dining area, etc.

Since Jasmine had a dedicated office in her current space, it would've been easy to try to shoehorn one into her new apartment. But visualizing the new space totally divorced from what she already had helped us open our minds to new possibilities that would work even better for her lifestyle. We decided she'd have a "mobile" office, storing her office needs in other areas of her apartment. For example, she could keep supplies in a kitchen cabinet, and store infrequently used files in the guest bedroom, then bring them to the kitchen table on the rare occasion she needed them.

This new vision influenced decisions on furniture to keep (or in this case, not keep) and what types of filing system we'd be using (in this case, clear plastic bins that allowed for hanging folders and a few accordion-style folders for mobility). And the same was true for the rest of the space: Creating a brand-new vision helped her identify which pieces of furniture she'd keep—and helped her let go of the rest.

We visualized what she'd be doing in her apartment to test our theories. When she came into her new apartment, where would she drop off her belongings? How would she sort through the mail? We had a vision, and this guided us. If we hadn't, she may have moved with a bunch of stuff she didn't need, but worse than that, she would've brought unproductive behaviors with her as well. In other words, she may have moved with ideas about the way things needed to be that were no longer so.

Regardless of whether you are modifying your current space or overhauling your living situation, allow yourself to imagine the process without too many constraints—just alignment with all your *whys* and priorities.

Create your vision

The format of your vision is not important: It can be an essay, a vision board, a roughly drawn sketch, a list of keywords, etc. This is more of a thinking exercise, but it'll help to have something tangible in front of you. If it also helps you, you can create a short-term vision (one to three years) and a longer-term vision.

Like Jasmine did, try to design instead of redesigning. Play a trick on your mind and put aside what you own. Only consider including the things you would want if you were starting from scratch, and the things that would help you reach your goal state. In other words, pretend your current home and stuff is a store. You can take things from this store for free. Here you are defining the needs you have and "designing" a solution. The good news is that 80 percent of your design is simply determining what items you no longer need in your home.

Your vision can be more senses-based. Consider what your new minimalist lifestyle *feels* like. What images, colors, and smells pop up? Spend time here thinking, noting, and sketching.

Or, your vision can be more functionality-based, like Jasmine's. Sketch out, either with images or words, the elements that connect your priorities to your physical space. We don't know the exact mechanics of the systems you'll be putting in place, nor the number or types of objects you'll retain (and any you may add). It's not necessary at this stage. With your list of priorities, focus on functions that relate to your home and even ones that don't.

For example, if becoming healthier is a priority and you know you prefer working out at a gym and riding your bike on a nearby trail, you don't need to dedicate any space in your home to exercise. You can sell the exercise equipment you have and use the money for bike gear. You'll also note that cooking healthy meals at home will mean that you need a kitchen that allows for regular meal planning, a clean and organized refrigerator, enough cleared-off counter space, and a review of kitchen appliances and equipment. Probably a cleared-off table to eat on as well. Being specific about your intentions in greater detail than "healthy activities" will make the visualization process more accurate but also simple and directed.

Your vision can be used to double-check your intentions, goals, and priorities. If we say that our top two priorities are exercise and spending more time with family but our visualization has a media center with video games and movies and a television in every room, but no space for exercise equipment, we know we need to tweak our visualization. If one of your priorities is to reduce stress, and your visualization includes an amorphous meditation space with images of candles and a yoga mat rolled out, you know that you're on the right track.

How do I know my vision is complete?
Like all blueprints, this one will evolve as you get into the downsizing process. Downsizing is like an excavation and inevitably results in "a-ha" moments you won't expect. This work always results in self-discovery, and we always uncover things we didn't know we had.

As such, you may need a bit more information about yourself and your feelings about things before getting into this level of detail of your vision.

Feel free to pause your vision creation at any point. You can keep it broad as you start your project, especially if it's a big one, and consider that complete for the time being so you can move on to the next step (creating a project plan). Don't let perfection be the enemy of the good.

Create a Project Plan

It's time to outline the steps you'll take to make these decisions real and gather some related resources. A project plan doesn't need to be tedious or complex. However, going through the downsizing process can be time-consuming, involving many ideas, resources, items to track, and tasks. A project plan will reduce decision fatigue, lessen stress about the work ahead, decrease opportunities to forget things, and clarify how to achieve tasks. It also allows us to highlight critical path items. These are decisions and tasks that must be completed to complete other tasks. It's essential to start with *something*, so I urge you not to skip this part.

Format

You can use whatever format works best for you. Piggyback on apps or software you already use. If you are allergic to spreadsheets, avoid them. Basic lists often work well, or even a simple table in a word processing document or notes app. A digital-based plan is easiest as you move things around or update and the easiest format to hyperlink or share with someone else. Regardless of your final plan's home, I suggest starting with a word processing document or spreadsheet in which you can dump thoughts and information. As the document grows, start categorizing the information and determining how to maintain it. The minimalist approach is to start simple and explore what is needed.

For my analog folks out there, a dedicated notebook can still be quite helpful, especially as thoughts and identification of tasks arise. Bring it along so you can write down anything that pops into your mind. Consider mixing your analog notes with digital to address different needs, even if it's only a list of relevant websites.

What to include

To begin with, you can include your intention, your vision, your *whys*, and any reminders or guiding principles picked up while reading this book. Then, add a task list. This can be general at first. Its central purpose is to house random tasks or projects that come up as you sort through your stuff (or that wake you up in the middle of the night).

Two other components are crucial steps in this process: a cursory inventory and decisions about what to do with unwanted items.

Cursory inventory

The purpose of this exercise is to physically investigate your space. Chances are you have things you don't know about. Your project plan will improve based on more data. By inventory, I don't mean a list of how many envelopes you own. Your cursory inventory should be general unless there's a specific and stressful category that you know will require a lot of attention. Note items of importance that live in multiple areas or that may be tricky rather than the stuff you know you'll remember and be thinking about.

When I mentioned this step during a talk I gave about Meaningful Minimalism, one of the attendees told me afterward that she thought of it as how she'd be *cursing* all the stuff she uncovered as she went through the downsizing process. We had a good laugh about it, but it reminded me of how daunting this step is for many of my clients. So try to think of it as an objective fact-finding mission and focus on the relief you'll feel afterward when you realize that the fear of "What's in there??" is gone. We want to minimize future surprise finds that may derail you.

As for the process itself, it may be easiest to think of in terms of areas or rooms in your home as categories to organize your inventory list. But you can categorize in any way that works best for you. It may be my stuff/their stuff, household items, hobbies, bedroom, furniture, memorabilia, for example. Whatever you choose, make sure it lines up with the way you categorize your stuff in your mind. And be sure to open any of those mystery boxes!

Make sure to list items that are not in your current home space. Otherwise known as your "hiding places." These are the places where you keep things you own but are not in your home itself. For example, your office, your friend's home, your car(s), a storage unit, a shed, or a second home. We tend to consider what we own to only be the stuff we hold in our living spaces. Without listing (or possibly remembering) the reach of our stuff-tentacles, we can't make more efficient and appropriate choices.

Our homes hold hiding places too. Occasionally we can bury something deeply: into a crawlspace, an attic, or a completely out-of-reach corner of a closet. Ignoring hiding places likely created some of your current problems to begin with, so while we need to identify them for the cursory inventory, it should highlight the importance of minimizing hiding places in the future.

An item should only exist outside of your home if it has a purpose in that specific place. For example, in your car you may need a phone charger, quarters, and jumper cables. You don't need camping gear, old flyers, or jackets. Storage units occasionally are needed for something very specific, like an artist's inventory, but not overflow or "I might need this one day when I have a bigger place" stuff.

As you go through this inventory, though, you'll start to see how a single category (whether more general or more specific) will have items scattered across multiple locations within and outside of your home. We'll address how to bring like items together in the How to "Do" Downsizing chapter.

What to do with unwanted items
When we start sorting through our stuff, it's easy to get derailed with

questions and tasks associated with where an unwanted item will go. We don't want it to be accidentally subsumed back into your stuff.

You may end up with some tasks for specific items like getting jewelry repaired or finding batteries for a device. Don't let these tasks linger or get swallowed back up. Some will be first steps. For example, if you want to keep something but it needs to be repaired. If it can't be repaired (or you don't want to pursue that route), the task of purchasing a new one needs to be added to your to-do list.

Identify big items like furniture or a vacuum cleaner or hard-to-retrieve items (e.g., behind boxes in the attic) that you want to let go of but at the moment of decision may not be able to easily throw into a donation bag. Or items you know you want to sell but don't want to gather up until you're ready to sell them. Add them to the list so you don't forget what to take to the donation center or forget the decision you already made. The list will be of these items and, in some cases, include the method of removal.

Begin a list of disposal options and any details that will make follow-through easier. Learn about all the recycling options your community offers, taking note of bulk trash pickup days and community shredding events. Think about what donation center(s) you'd like to use and make a decision about what you want to report and get credit for donating and have a system for tracking. Decide whether you want to sell any items, and if so, what selling sites and apps you feel comfortable using, etc.

The following are the primary types of disposal options to consider:

Recycling. No one recycles completely correctly. This is not your fault as the specifics around what can be recycled tend to be confusing. Read your local community's website detailing what is and isn't accepted, using this is an opportunity to learn more. But keep the adage in mind, "When in doubt, throw it out." It can be more detrimental to put items out for recycling that can't be recycled than vice versa.

Non-curbside recycling. Most communities have responsible disposal for household hazardous waste, electronics, and scrap metal. Sometimes paint and other specialty items are taken as well. Some even have paper-shredding events at these stations.

Reuse centers. If you are lucky enough to have such places near you, it's a great way to properly get rid of hardware, mirrors, tools, tiles, etc. There are also creative reuse centers that accept donations. These are great because they allow items that most donation centers won't accept.

Large charities. For unbroken, still useful items. Be sure to read the charity's website to learn what they accept. Pick one that is easy to get to, possibly on your way to other regular trips. Some will do pick-ups. This is especially helpful for furniture, but be aware that some pick-ups take a while to arrange.

Homeless or women's shelters and religious centers. Good-quality cold-weather clothes and gear, unopened toiletries, and unopened beauty products can be best used at a shelter or woman's support service nonprofit. Some organizations will take partially used toiletries as well.

Sell. If you want to sell a lot of items, consider keeping a list and breaking these up into different resale websites and apps. There may be a fair amount of money to be made in this process so take advantage of that if you have the time and financial need. There are many apps, especially for clothing, that can work well again, if the time (and potential disappointment) trade-off works for you. You may consider just focusing on selling a small number of items that have a higher potential price, or if it's fun for you to sell a bunch of clothes in good shape, have at it. Also, consider tracking the money made from this process if you want to use that amount to put toward new, good-quality items that you actually need.

Friends and family. It's great when we can give something to someone we know can use it. The trick is to not give them things they don't want or will feel guilty about. And you also have to remember to give it to them. Don't underestimate this as an additional task, even if at first it feels like a good idea to give things away to specific people. Be sure you have an easy plan to get it done. Add this to your calendar or leave items by your door when you have plans to see the recipient.

In the next chapter, you'll make each category physical, setting up bins or bags and getting to work!

How to "Do" Downsizing

It's time to get rid of stuff.

I've put this off as long as possible: We've gotten philosophical and turned inward toward our emotions. We've laughed, cried, and created a project plan. This means you're primed to say goodbye. Yes, the emotions will still arise, conundrums will still surface, and decision-making will be tiring, but hopefully you're incredibly excited!

While your mental perspective has (hopefully) shifted, you may not feel a sense of results. Your home space or room or office still looks the same. And you know there are things ... lurking. Now you are prepared, or as much as you can be, to start moving things around a bit. Start opening boxes taped closed for who knows how many years, investigating the contents of drawers, addressing forgotten things, and, most difficultly, evaluating the heart-wrenching stuff.

But first, a warning. One of the questions clients ask me before our first session is: "What should I buy?" That's because buying things to organize with is the fun and easy part of establishing a minimalist home. But resist the urge to buy anything as your initial downsizing will likely leave you with emptied bins and boxes and other sorting devices that can be repurposed until you've begun the organizing process—though you can add a list of potential purchases to the project plan as you think of them.

The setup

When beginning the paring-down process, set up boxes, containers, or bags to organize the "leaving the house" part. The only things you may need to purchase are painter's tape and permanent markers for labeling, but be sure to look around first to see if you have these! Also, big contractor bags are more sturdy than regular trash bags, so aside from using what you already have, a box of these can be helpful.

Decide how much you care about what happens to items you release based on the time you have to devote to this project, the convenience of drop-off points, and your finances. Use the categories listed in the previous chapter to get you started and further fill out your project plan where needed.

The setup step can be a bit tricky if you're in a small space. In that case, only start setting things up when you're ready to work.

Adjust your mindset to allow for more (controlled) chaos before things get better. Remember that it's a temporary frustration for a long-lasting, meaningful solution.

Creating categories of stuff

The cardinal rule of organizing is to bring like items together. Of course, there are exceptions when the sheer volume is cumbersome or if the items are spread out in different places, thereby making this strategy logistically challenging. This is where having a cursory inventory of all that you own can be a helpful support. Perhaps it's going straight for the heart and sitting with an old family member's keepsakes. Keep in mind that you'll be moving stuff around a bit as you recategorize in your mind. You won't know exactly what the categories are from the beginning and how granular you want to become in your sorting. Categorization is iterative too.

Your categories will be dependent on your project scope and whether others in your household participate in this venture. I urge you not to simply use rooms as categories, although you'll start this way until you come across items with cousins in other rooms. Even if they will eventually be dispersed, you'll still need to bring those together.

Let's look at a simple example: flashlights. Gather up all your flashlights. I mean all of them, even from your car and the basement. Now, think about your use cases for flashlights. What is the real need here? Does the power go out? How often? When it does, do you just use the flashlight on your phone? Are there some cases where you need a larger, more powerful flashlight? Do you end up just using candles during power outages? Once you've determined what you need, pick only those flashlights out from the pile.

Let's say you keep three out of six. You've chosen these three because they meet your size requirements and have proven, perhaps, to be more reliable than the others. You double-check them to ensure they are still working and make sure you have extra batteries available. During this process, you may find that you actually do need to buy a new flashlight because the one that meets an important need is broken. Or, you may realize that, while several flashlights are broken, they don't need to be replaced because they didn't fit your use cases and were, therefore, unneeded extras.

While you're generally trying to avoid having multiples of an item, especially when there are minimal differences, it's actually better to have multiples in situations where it makes life notably easier and serves a specific purpose—like having a flashlight on each floor for easy access if the power goes out.

The category approach allows you to see your stuff from a different vantage point. It may result in creating subcategories, which can help you get rid of large groups of items at once, organize the items you keep, and reduce the number of decisions you need to make. While bringing items into categories, you may even quickly identify items to go and immediately drop them into the appropriate box in your setup area, which is set up for items leaving your home.

How to start letting go of objects
Did you feel a moment of panic?

Your project plan includes a running list of what to do with the stuff. But you still need to pick up an item and make a decision. But how to actually *start*? With all this buildup, we don't want to put too much pressure on your first actions.

In one day, you can do just one thing. Then you've gotten over the mental hurdle of starting. You've dipped your toe in the water to test its temperature. Some like to dive straight in, while others prefer the slow steps in, wincing at key moments.

Sometimes it's best to start with the low-hanging fruit of your situation. Perhaps the closet full of clothes seems the most contained. Maybe it's leaving the living space of your home to address the half-used cans of paint and never-used power tools in the garage.

Whatever it takes to get started, remember what Nike says: "Just do it."

Kill your darlings

Since I'm writing a book, I might as well offer a book metaphor. "Kill your darlings" is a writing strategy in which an author cuts sentences or storylines that they've worked hard on for the sake of the overall story. It's difficult because the writing might be excellent or a lot of time was spent on developing the content. But it needs to be deleted, however good, in service to the final piece of writing.

This strategy can be applied to your stuff as well. Just because you let something go doesn't mean that it never meant anything to you, that it isn't a great product or piece of art or that the person who gave you that item isn't important to you.

Recognizing that you are killing your darlings makes it easier to do. Acknowledge the love you have for your items. But for the sake of a simpler, more meaningful life, and to reach your goals, you'll have to let go of things you love but that no longer fit.

This reminds me of the story of Warren Buffet, as retold by Oliver Burkeman, in his book *Four Thousand Weeks: Time Management for Mortals.*[5] Buffet is asked by his pilot how to set priorities. Buffet tells him to list, ordered from most important to least, his top twenty-five priorities in life. He advises the pilot to organize his time around the top five. But instead of suggesting that the remaining twenty are things to do with any remaining time, he suggests deleting them entirely. Their existence on any list would act as a distractor, even unconsciously, and simply aren't important enough to make the cut, so why let them linger?

The problem with *perfects* and *almost perfects*

Similar to killing your darlings, we heavily weigh all of the positive attributes of an item without stepping back to look at the bigger problem. There are devices, objects, and tools that seem to be "the perfect thing for the perfect time." These are tempting to keep for obvious reasons but can result in you owning more items than you need without life getting notably easier. That's when taking a step back will strategically help you ascertain whether the "perfect thing for the perfect time" is worthwhile. Often, a slightly lesser or different type of "tool" will do the job just fine.

---

5 Oliver Burkeman, *Four Thousand Weeks: Time Management for Mortals* (New York: Farrar, Straus and Giroux, 2021), p. 77.

Also, it's incredibly difficult to let go of things that feel *almost* perfect. That super-cool shirt you found when traveling that looks amazing on you … but feels uncomfortable so you rarely wear it. Sometimes *almost perfects* are not items but people in our lives or activities that are mostly amazing but have a red-flag drawback.

Seeing past the sentimental

Sentimentality can be misplaced when we feel uncomfortable letting go of something that is really old. We place a particular value on some items simply because of their age. This is reinforced by programs like *Antiques Roadshow* that highlight the hidden treasures stashed in our homes. If selling items you believe are valuable interests you, take the time to do it. But if you're holding onto these items thinking they are worth top dollar, but you haven't taken action, consider whether you're willing to put the time into pursuing your belief.

Many of us view photos as precious, family heirlooms as sacrosanct, and consider anything that evokes a memory as worth keeping. As a result, we find it difficult to let go of anything connected to our past. Usually, guilt arises when considering letting go of items given to us or that may be family-related, including kids' childhood stuff (e.g., art projects, baby clothes, trinkets). Other emotions come up too: feelings of responsibility to carry a family torch or allow items with historical relevance to persist, or resistance to letting go of one's past identity. Of course, holding onto a family heirloom that you use on special occasions is special and sweet. But you don't need a lot of these; pick your favorites.

I've worked with clients who have kept old family photos for decades that had been passed on to them from an older relative. They've never looked at them and shuffle them from one closet corner to another. Often, they don't know most of the people in the photos. They could pull out the few they recognize, but the process feels overwhelming. So the default is to keep. But it doesn't need to be. The truth is, they can throw out the whole box in a single moment, and nothing in their life would change except for a small weight lifted. But it feels uncomfortable because printed photos are considered precious, as they capture a moment in time.

Being nostalgic can provoke moments of sweet longing and deep memory. Such reactions to nostalgic objects are perfectly human. However, it becomes a problem when we hold onto stuff purely because it elicits nostalgia. Nostalgia, for nostalgia's sake, keeps too much of our past in our present, especially when there is nothing more profound underneath it. Nostalgia doesn't carry with it its own intrinsic meaning. It may seem at first glance to be meaningful. But it's not the kind of meaning we're trying to build in our minimalist lifestyle.

All the family history we hold onto in the form of material goods, or those we think others want to hold onto of ours once we pass, are nice to have. But true meaning lies in these relationships. Relationships never die. You can be both drowning in your grandmother's old stuff while hesitant to give your own things away in case your kids want it. This is normal. Start to find the balance here.

Piles of shame

While your *darlings* and your *almost perfects* are typically things that would feel good to keep, *piles of shame* are things we keep even though they make us feel bad. These are items that remind us of bad times in our lives, perceived failures, problematic people, and mistakes. Sometimes these are the things we hold onto most tightly. Sometimes our home is essentially a pile of shame. Shame can exist so deeply that we often don't know it's there. We might not even know it's the cause of our actions or, in the case of minimalism, inaction.

We talked about letting go of guilt and shame in the Transform Guilt into Gratitude chapter. Sometimes that's a lifelong process. But we don't have a lifetime to work on the major overhaul of your home at this moment. To overcome piles of shame, first identify them as such. It may not be evident until you feel resistance to letting go of certain things that you know you don't specifically enjoy or have to retain for a clear but functional reason. Unpack and sort through them physically and then unpack them emotionally. Because this is a deep-rooted feeling, talking to someone or journaling can help. Then consider the practical or logical steps that will help you let go of the item. Once this has been identified, see if you're ready to take action. If not yet, think about what it would take to be ready, and at the very least, note this task on your project plan.

Not a solitary sport

We may feel more alone than ever in the overwhelming space of our personal histories, emptied boxes, and piles of shame.

In fact, the whirlwind of stuff, to-dos, and events keep us from confronting the edges of our loneliness. We consume information about minimalism and organizing alone, through podcasts, blogs, social media scrolls, and shows.

Minimalism is not a solitary sport. Or at least it doesn't have to be. Consider sharing your experiences and learn from others. Your community and network not only influence what you own but also how you manage the items you release. This includes the grocery store that collects plastic bags for recycling, your Buy Nothing Group, and the local consignment shop. You're not alone.

We don't need to keep that used-once-a-year pie pan because our neighbor next door is an avid baker and they'd be happy to lend one. We don't need the rarely used tools because our public library includes a tool library. We have a great place to donate used office and art supplies so those in need have them available, including teachers looking to supplement school supplies for students. We take our used batteries that are scattered around to the local transfer station that accepts household hazardous waste. We take, borrow, and give back.

You can enlist an accountability buddy or have a friend with a penchant for organizing come over one night for takeout and to help go through all your books. You can even have a friend over to sit and catch up with you as you complete mundane tasks. You can hire an extra pair of hands, as needed, to help with easy-to-direct tasks like moving things around or organizing and delivering your unwanted items. You can even hire a professional organizer or a minimalist coach.

While we've examined how other people can be used as excuses not to do this work, they can also be great supporters of your efforts.

Prepare for some (more) chaos

Paring down can become more complicated when you see that the state of your home seems to have gotten messier. It gets worse before it gets better. You'll be engaging in a lot of uncovering and gathering of things that will converge into piles dotting your home. This is a time to be strategic but also embrace a bit of chaos. Excavation can be organized while looking messy. This is where patience and trust in the process come in.

While you shouldn't get up every time you need to bring an item to another area in your home, you can create piles or baskets of items to be redistributed, then put the items away when the piles get unruly, you've completed your day's work, or you need a quick break.

If you have next steps for certain items, get those moving as soon as you can without disrupting your process. If you're going through Christmas stockings and want to know if your sister wants the one your great-grandmother crocheted, send that text in the moment to get the ball rolling and avoid forgetting or needing to add something else to your to-do list. Once you receive a response, you can determine where it goes, avoiding more chaos.

Prioritize follow-through

Sometimes the last 1 percent of a project becomes the hardest, even though you've completed the most difficult work. Never underestimate the importance of labeling, closing bags, and bringing them to their ultimate destinations. That's when the freedom from your stuff will really be felt.

If it frustrates you to toss something in the trash or even in the recycling bin or charity box, don't use it as an excuse to keep an item you no longer need or will never use. You're only delaying the inevitable. It's good that it frustrates you. Remember *landfill purgatory*.

Don't stash items you no longer want out of sight, where they might be forgotten about. Employ various strategies like hanging bags on the front door so you won't forget on the way out, scheduling a bulk trash pickup, or putting donation drop-off days on your calendar and project plan. Avoid the common misstep of loading bags in your car and driving around with them for months before dropping them off.

Focusing on the final step of removal will also prevent the chaos from swallowing the items marked for removal back in. It'll energize your work with the relief of that stuff being gone. Don't let your efforts be in vain because you don't prioritize following through.

Finally, a major paring-down problem occurs when the number of decisions starts to become ominous, annoying, and complicated. We'll deep-dive into how to combat decision fatigue to assuage these frustrations and continue moving forward.

Combat Decision Fatigue

Downsizing and organizing projects, no matter how seemingly small, involves a series of cascading decisions. Most are mundane, many are tiring or tricky, and some are emotionally weighted. No wonder most people quit partway through the downsizing process.

We want to prepare for decision-making before being faced with it in the moment. We want to set things up as well as possible from a logistics point of view and have some decision-making shortcuts in place. We've already done some of the mental and emotional preparation for this in previous sections. And we want to do it to help prevent decision fatigue and make better choices.

It's okay to have feelings. They are inputs (if they have staying power) but not the decision-makers. As Susan David, author of

Emotional Agility, reminds us, "Feelings are data, not decisions." So when you're faced with cascading decisions, be careful how your emotions are tangled up in them. Considering and then unpacking your feelings *are* part of the process, but they're not the end result.

Be prepared for cascading decisions

Beginning a project with the acknowledgment that you will be confronted with a stream of decision points is best. Understand that one decision may hinge upon the next. You may be starting small and then expand when you move one item into another room to, let's say, put it on a shelf, only to discover that said shelf is packed too tightly and you need to remove items from it. In doing so, you rediscover a book left by an old friend you always meant to return. But finding their address is difficult because they moved recently, and you only have their old one. You don't want to reach out because a phone call will eat up another hour. You know they take a long time to respond to emails and don't want to wait because now your living room has piles on the floor, and you know you won't be able to make it to the donation center for two weeks, and you don't have a large staging area. These pesky, relentless decisions have cascaded down, and you give up. That's one way that disorganization happens and stays that way: the paralyzing nature of too many decisions.

Pick a time to organize when you know you have some wiggle room if things go awry. Build in some minutes at the end of your session to clean up. Utilize your setup area and keep your task list on hand for next steps.

Decisions can be sticky but don't let yourself get stuck. Get into the mindset and rhythm of decisiveness, even if that's not your proclivity. Attitude is something you can adjust alongside proper planning. It gets easier the more you do it, and with all the little decisions you make, you are sure to get in your practice.

Don't worry about making mistakes

As we discussed in the Decision-Making as a Skill chapter, we stress over the risk of not making the right decision. This is a lesson that not only applies to the downsizing and organizing process but also all elements of decision-making about your lifestyle. This is based on the idea that there is a right or wrong decision to be made. We believe the right/wrong mental construct is worth it because we might make the right choice, the payoff of which would make everything perfect. But there is no perfect.

A right or wrong decision doesn't exist in the first place. There are too many external, unpredictable variables; too many ways in which a person may change and grow. You have limited information today and you can't predict the future.

By admitting to the flaw in the construct and therefore relinquishing the attachment to making the right decision, we can de-emphasize mistakes. If you get caught up in the right or wrong decision game, you will be more stressed, take less action, and probably not make better decisions than you would have otherwise.

Do your best and move on. The types of decisions you'll be making will mostly be low-stakes. Most won't involve making large commitments or completely altering the trajectory of your life. Most will be shirts, kitchen tools, and shreddable paperwork that won't involve particularly detrimental results if a "mistake" is made.

Multiple passes and maybe piles

When dealing with a category of items (e.g., clothes) or a room in your home (e.g., a bathroom), it's reasonable to take multiple passes. Meaning, you go through most or everything once and then on another day come back to the project with fresh eyes to review and get rid of more items.

The mini version of multiple passes is the "maybe pile." As you sort items, you are likely creating "keep" and "goodbye" piles before they are redistributed. This allows for the opportunity to create maybe piles. These are items you're not so sure about, but to keep going through items, you set them aside here so you can take another pass at reviewing them.

These two strategies work best with highly emotional items and large categories that feel too overwhelming for quick decisions. Making an initial cut to lower emotional pressure and reduce the volume can make the process easier to handle. Decision fatigue can arrive as we make harder decisions, so taking a break can alleviate the pressure enough to allow you to make all the difficult decisions in one go.

But while both these techniques can be useful, they are a slippery slope that can result in your minimalism project never getting done or overthinking. They may end up being unintended procrastination techniques. To avoid this, consider noting how many passes you want to take as part of your project planning. And do the same for maybe piles.

Only pick out what you want to keep

You can pick out what you want to keep from each category and then let go of everything else wholesale. This is a quicker strategy and will help avoid a lot of the *what-if-ing* and rationalizing that we tend to do. It also helps do away with a lot of picking through smaller items and minutiae if you're not at risk of accidentally letting go of something you really might need.

Defaulting to "don't keep" can be a more efficient and effective strategy to avoid the cascading decisions problem.

Take a photo or put it on a list—but be careful

You may realize while going through your stuff that you're keeping an item to remember something, even when you don't actually want to keep it. Basically, the problem is that you don't want to forget. A common solution for this is to take a picture of the item or put it on a relevant list. This is a great way to keep the memory rather than the physical object you were using to remind yourself. Sometimes these actions make it easier to make the final decision to let go of something.

But beware: It can be a slippery slope of disorganized and forgotten-about photos or notes that only add to your digital overload, so be sure to create an organized repository that you won't forget about, and, of course, be very selective about what it holds.

Identify whether it's a consumable or an object

Note when something is a consumable, like a candle, dishwasher detergent, or toilet paper, versus an object like a clock or a couch. The fact that the consumables can be used up doesn't make them unimportant to review or potentially get rid of. Consumables should not get a free pass. But there is more middle ground with them. You may decide not to purchase that particular consumable again, but you may like it enough to decide that it's worth keeping "temporarily" as it's used up to save money or because you will still get something out of having it before it's completely gone.

In-betweens like Swedish dishcloths also last for months but are eventually composted. Or items like underwear should be replaced more often than a pair of jeans.

Create rulesets and heuristics

Emotional attachment and decision fatigue make it hard to make good decisions in the moment. That's where rulesets and heuristics become handy. Within the context of downsizing, rulesets are a set of parameters determining what you keep and what you let go of. For example, when you're getting ready to purge your closet, you might create a ruleset that says you'll get rid of something you haven't worn in one year, if it doesn't fit properly, or if it's damaged beyond your ability to repair in under an hour. Defining those rules ahead of time makes it easier to address each piece of clothing.

Heuristics are mental shortcuts or rules of thumb to reduce cognitive load and make more efficient decisions. Some heuristics you might be familiar with—and might even have used—are letting something go if it makes you feel bad about yourself, or saving items related to legal or governmental matters. These heuristics help us make a quick judgment, which is appropriate for many basic downsizing decisions. Please note: Used generally in life, heuristics can be problematic, leading to inaccurate conclusions. Be careful to use them only when the stakes are low!

Creating rules and heuristics ahead of time will make each decision simpler and help you avoid letting emotions derail you. Remember that emotions are inputs; they shouldn't be the driver of your decision-making. If you are still stuck in emotional attachment, each decision related to that attachment will take more energy. That's why we try to address the emotions when we're not sitting in front of the items themselves and why we've been doing all this pre-work and planning. Rulesets will give you a bit of distance from the emotions that may arise and save you time too. You can write these up as a companion document to your project plan to solidify your approach.

Rulesets and heuristics can be created in a variety of ways. Besides lack of use and damage, you may choose to let go of anything you're keeping out of guilt. You may determine a replacement cost threshold if that makes you more comfortable letting go of low-cost items you don't otherwise want to keep. If you tend to keep things out of concern over the slight chance you might have to rebuy them in the future, this can be an effective strategy.

A ruleset around books could be, "I will use the library for books from now on. I will only keep books that I use for reference and that I haven't read yet. I will donate all other books to the library because giving back to my community is an important priority in my life."

You can create specific rulesets for as many categories as are appropriate. For example, you might decide to limit person-based memorabilia to only one or two items from each relative or friend. You might create another ruleset for a category like socks, letting go of all without matches, with holes, and knee-highs. Some rulesets can be created in advance while others may come up in the moment. For example, creating rulesets is very important for paperwork, though you will likely have to start sifting through it before you can finalize your ruleset to get a sense of what you'll be dealing with.

While rulesets and heuristics are meant to preempt emotions, it doesn't mean creating them will prevent emotions from coming up at all. However, they are less likely to arise and will be less strong if you're not in a panic mode or dealing with decision fatigue that's threatening to consume you while sorting through items. If used mindfully, rulesets and heuristics will become your best friend as you downsize.

Stuff eulogy

The process of letting go, whether it be of a dear relationship, an old identity, or a bunch of your stuff, involves *grieving*. It's helpful to be aware of this so you can be prepared. If you feel grief of any sort starting to scratch at your heart, deal with it. And if that means bringing people into your process, do so. A *stuff eulogy* is where you speak aloud to someone (a friend, family member, professional organizer) the meaning an item has held in your life and how you are now ready to let it go.

I worked with a septuagenarian client, Jane, who was focused on some serious downsizing. To create ease for her children and grandchildren, she solidified her will and let go of countless bags of stuff, keeping only what she needs and that enriches her life. Her efforts will segue into an out-of-state (or country!) move for her next phase now that she's retired. This process has allowed methodical and mindful sorting, in her full mental and physical capacity, never feeling rushed or stressed. She's been determined and focused and took the time to say goodbye to once-treasured items.

Goodbyes of all types are challenging, even when we think *Good riddance!* or are excited about where we're headed. Whether it's people or places or things, they all hold something, which may make it complicated to let go. Sometimes this leads to us holding onto more later because we don't want to re-experience the regret of goodbye. When we ignore goodbyes, the buildup of the unacknowledged but related emotions catch up with us as repressed feelings that pop up unexpectedly. Mostly, we miss an opportunity to get to know ourselves better.

Saying goodbye completely alone is an added challenge. That's why funerals aren't solo events. It's why we externally process difficult emotions and sort through complex situations with people we trust. But we often don't engage with others during the significant goodbyes that we experience with our stuff. Even if living with a partner, there may be more contention or less patience with these farewells. Sometimes calling a friend or family member can help, though there's always the risk of them steering us back toward keeping the item.

Back to my client: She began telling me about some pivotal papers she'd written during her career and how they related to her mentor (who'd passed away). As she was describing them—what they meant to her and why she was ready to let them go—I said, "It sounds like you've come to a decision." She said, "I guess I have." But it took saying it aloud and to someone who understood and supported her decision to move on. I explained that even once we've (mostly) decided to part with an item, we need to recite its eulogy and have someone witness it. This also provides a level of accountability. The "stuff eulogy" isn't needed for most items, but it makes a difference for stickier ones and ensures that we don't default to keeping items.

I have another client, Jon, who said, "I think I'm ready to let these things go. I just need you to bless the decision." Alone, he would have defaulted to resisting the donation bag. It's almost always easier to keep than to let go. I listened to the stories of the items, reconfirming his analysis and adding to the reasons why it was time to let go. I saw the way this eased his mind and quickened the process. He needed the eulogy and the extra ease of me directing what to do with the items (e.g., donate, sell, recycle) to avoid becoming distracted by another decision to make. He could focus on the emotional end of the process that proved to be cathartic.

The stuff eulogy is an effective tool in the downsizing process. It acknowledges this work's emotional component while reminding us that minimalism doesn't need to be a solitary sport. Grief is nonlinear, so while acknowledging grief at this stage is essential, it will weave in and out; allow it.

Decision fatigue toolbox

Even with your decision-making strategies, you still need to have a "toolbox" ready for moments of decision fatigue. This may include the following:

- Do a physical activity like taking a walk to release your frustrated energy.
- Talk to someone or journal to work through your thoughts.
- Take a real break and pick up your work the next day.
- Give yourself helpful reminders like "I don't always need the perfect thing at the perfect time," and "I can't make the wrong decision."

These strategies will help you navigate through the onslaught of decision-making. They will be buoyed by the work you completed in previous sections about your intentions, priorities, and even your initial *whys*.

Make It a Fun, Feel-Good Experience

Make it feel good

In previous chapters, we've looked at decision-making from different angles: saying no to the status quo, questioning organization and optimization, rationalizations and *what-ifs*, behavioral economics, trade-offs, delayed gratification, etc. These are all useful strategies, especially when enacted in concert. But it can consume our thinking too much. Occasionally, the most practical decision isn't the best one. If you're buying a car, you have to be mindful of price and safety, but while choosing between two that meet these parameters, you might choose the less practical one because it just *feels good*.

Also, sometimes, it's okay to keep a silly trinket because it makes us smile every time we look at it. Being tough on ourselves with other, more impactful stuff leaves us room for some "just because" items.

Remember, we're doing this to create space for the special stuff. When paring down, it's easy to get lost in decisions around stuff you're getting rid of. Sure, you have your priorities and intentions to guide you, but the purpose of letting things go is to have the things you really want and make them more prominent in your home and lifestyle. Your work is to create a simple backdrop so that you can emphasize the special things in life, even if they are material in nature.

When we find ourselves digging deep into a downsizing project, getting our financials in order, and creating clear systems to keep our lives flowing efficiently, we must call on that internal compass to help us make some final decisions. While we may be positioned to make great decisions, we need to feel directed and confident in making them. We don't have to drive ourselves crazy.

Remember not to stress over the risk of not making the right decision, as discussed in the Decision-Making as a Skill chapter. Happiness and stress reduction will elude you if you don't take the time to know yourself intimately and, in doing so, have the ability and kindness to make your life feel good.

When we are trying to get everything to fit just right, it's important to hear these words: "Do what you are comfortable with." Because in the end, nurturing your relationship with yourself, within the context of personal growth, is the sweet spot of making it feel good. It is your home; it is your life. It should feel good.

Make it fun

If all that wasn't enough, sometimes a gimmick, trick, or something more fun can flip our perspective on a project like this. The following are a few ideas to get you started:

Un-warming party. You've heard of a housewarming party. How about an un-warming party? Instead of bringing things into your home, friends and family can come over to celebrate your incredible downsizing accomplishments. Leave out items you no longer need for them to take. And don't let the name fool you. With friends and family around, you'll be reminded of the most important, and warmest, objects of life—the people you care about.

Old-school garage sale. These are great if the emphasis is not on making a lot of money. Focus on meeting neighbors, and make it joyful with snow cones or lemonade. Include items that you think will earn a few dollars or that might be more difficult to donate. Only be a tough negotiator on prices if that's fun for you.

Fashion show. When there are a bunch of clothes in the maybe pile, get dolled up and have friends over for a fashion show. Even better if these friends are bluntly honest and have a good fashion sense. They can help you decide which clothing, shoes, and accessories to keep or give away as you walk a makeshift runway.

Fake shopping. Think of your home as a store and go shopping for what you really want and then "return" the items you no longer desire by donating or selling them.

Pizza party trick. Invite unsuspecting friends over for a pizza party (or whatever food and drink is most enticing) and have them help you go through your stuff. This is best if you need physical assistance or the accountability that comes with their presence. Straightforward bribery works too.

Gamify. Make this a game! You can use the amount of time, the number of bags, or another component as a basis for the game. Maybe set a goal amount for how much money you want to make selling your stuff and then spend part of that amount on one item or activity you really want as a prize.

Principles of Organizing

As we discussed in the Questioning Organization, Optimization, and Productivity chapter, the primary strategy of this work is to simplify, not organize. However, organizing is one of your simplification tools. Since you're developing your own version of minimalism, that means you'll have your own version of organization.

Some specific organizing strategies will work for some people but be terribly problematic for others. Also, any organization strategy should be specific to the problem you're attempting to solve. The clearer you are about the problem, the more likely you'll be able to identify an effective organizing solution. The details of organizing are highly specific to your stuff, home space, and needs.

While I can't offer prescriptive approaches for your unique situation, the following concepts apply to almost everyone.

Organizing levels

Much like how it's difficult to decorate and buy furniture for a new home until you've lived there for a bit, you don't need to complete organization right away. Organizing has levels. The top is the general "where." Your house, car, garage? Using earplugs as an example: Starting with the general "where," you might decide you need to keep them in your bedroom, because you use them to sleep. Narrowing down, consider with what other objects they should be kept (i.e., objects needed right before bed). Then, think through the specific place (i.e., nightstand) and where within that place (i.e., top drawer on the left). Finally, assess whether there's additional organizing needed. In the case of earplugs, you might want to place them inside a small jar so they are protected and don't get lost.

You don't have to go through these levels all at once. You may pause at any point until you have enough lifestyle data to determine how to tweak and finalize, and you can always test different strategies.

Begin with the end in mind

While you should wait until you've mostly downsized before focusing on organizing, it's helpful to think about how you'll organize and create systems as you pare down your stuff. In conjunction with the vision you created, think about how you want your space to look in the end.

Consider how you'll engage with the items you've chosen to keep. This may inform whether it's worth keeping an item or highlight the importance of organizing a category of items well. It's also helpful to loosely organize things as you work. But don't let yourself get too distracted by coming up with a final organization solution. You may find down the road that a different strategy is needed.

Determine your mess tolerance

Mathematically, I've deduced that it takes at least ten times as long to organize a mess than to create one. So when you're organizing, think about how you'll maintain your newfound organization once things inevitably get out of place. We all have different tolerance windows and time that we can allot to tidying up. Consider the amount and type of unruliness you can handle without feeling too stressed or overwhelmed. Think ahead to what your tidying routine will look like. Then, attempt to solve for the biggest problems you foresee happening frequently.

For example, you may want all the kids' toys you keep in the kitchen to be beautifully organized, but since they are constantly being used and may be dangerous if left on the floor (little pieces you could trip on or that the dog may mistake for food), you opt for a basic bin system that allows you (or kiddo!) to put things away quickly. Over time you'll adjust as you notice what stuff causes the most problems when it's out of place and what stuff is the most difficult or time-consuming to put back in its home.

Try to keep categories together

In addition to bringing like items together during the downsizing process, you'll use similar categories during the organization process. But now you'll go a step further, moving from more general categories like clothing, books, paperwork, kitchen items, electronics, personal care items, and toys and games into subcategories. For example, clothes have shirts and pants as subcategories and types of shirts as a subcategory within shirts. You can keep subcategorizing until you hit a point of diminishing returns. (It may not be helpful to subdivide your tee shirts into stripes and solids, for example.)

When items in the same category live in different places, you risk forgetting what you have in aggregate. Start with the hypothesis that these categories will be kept together, keeping in mind that there are common situations when that makes less sense. Like when the same type of items is used in different rooms, such as throw blankets. Other items, however, can all be organized in one central place and then taken out and used as needed, like cleaning supplies in a utility closet.

It's best to err on the side of more general categories to de-dupe items with the same functionality and question the smaller differences between items. For example, you might consider cleaning supplies as one big category, depending on how large your home is and the different types of cleaning supplies you use. Or you might break them into different groups based on which areas they clean (bathroom, kitchen), whether they're objects like a vacuum cleaner versus consumable liquids like multipurpose spray. But avoid maintaining duplicates or multiple items with overlapping functionality, even if you organize based on the room they are used in rather than a more general cleaning category.

My client Eve was clearing out a bunch of her stuff. She realized that she tended to organize by periods in her life or things she got from certain people rather than basic categories like clothes, artwork, kitchen stuff, etc. This scattered her things more than they already were and made the task of going through her stuff and organizing it for a move more difficult. The work became more manageable once she understood how to reframe her categories.

Organize based on how you use things

As with all rules, some are meant to be broken. It may seem at odds with keeping categories of things together, but this speaks to decision-making hierarchy. You first try to organize by category but change gears when you know that something won't work well for you. There are no hard and fast rules about how a home *should* be organized. It's organized if it's easy for you to manage and makes your life easier.

In the end, all these organized components are going to be a part of the systems you employ. When you organize your hall closet, think about how you use the items in it and how they may interact with other items in your home. You may keep all of your dog supplies on one shelf in your pantry, but the leash and poop bags need to stay by the door for ease of access.

I've walked into so many clients' homes and immediately been able to see that they'd hired professional organizers before. I can usually see the artifacts of what the organizer did. It's never that they did a poor job; it's that they weren't taking into account the very specific needs and personality of the person they were working for and neglected to create systems that would allow the client to continuously care for their more organized space.

Organizing for yourself, not how you think you're supposed to, is paramount to creating simple systems.

Everything has a home

After gathering similar items during the categorization and paring down processes, remaining items must be reorganized throughout your space. (Hopefully, items now have more obvious homes because you've thought about each one and intentionally kept it for a specific purpose.) By home, I don't mean a general room or corner of a room. I'm talking about an exact home; the specific place the item will clearly return to if you temporarily move it. I'm talking about the small jar where the earplugs are stored in the left side of the top drawer of the nightstand. This will come in handy when you're in maintenance mode. Putting things away is annoying, but it's far less so when you know the exact place to put the thing.

Everyone in your home should be aware of these new homes too. My dad was in constant confusion when I was growing up because my mom was always moving things around but never telling him. Part of keeping everything in order is ensuring everyone knows what the order is.

Determine the impetus for retrieval

Everything we own can't be visible and easily accessible. Because of this, we need to keep the impetus for retrieval in mind when looking for an item's home. An impetus for retrieval is the event or situation that triggers the need to take out the item.

Some items have a clear impetus for retrieval and are used often; those, we want to be easily accessible. If you drink coffee every morning, you have a consistent impetus for retrieval. You will never forget where your coffee is. Even if you didn't make it easily accessible, you'd still know exactly where to get it. But, of course, it would be silly to put it somewhere hard to get because of its frequency of use.

Some items have a clear impetus for retrieval but are used less frequently, so they can be kept somewhere more challenging to reach like in the back of a closet; for example, ski equipment for a twice-a-year ski trip. In this case, you know you have the ski equipment and need to take it with you on the ski trip, but since you only need to grab it a few times when packing for a trip, it's okay if it takes time to retrieve it.

Some items have an unlikely or unclear impetus for retrieval—like an extra appliance part that you rarely need or some memorabilia you've tucked away in the attic—so you need to establish a way to remember that you have the item and an easy way to access it (a Post-it note on the back of the appliance reminding you where that rarely needed part is, or a digital inventory of what's in the attic). Keep in mind, though, that it should be a rare exception to keep something that has a low impetus for retrieval and low accessibility, if at all.

No junk drawer or miscellaneous category

Junk drawers are defeatist in nature. The term "junk" hides the nature of the drawer's contents and makes finding things more difficult. Sort of like using the term "clutter." There's a laziness to it that obscures the underlying issues.

Similarly, organizing items into a "miscellaneous" category is problematic. Labeling something miscellaneous does not promote wayfinding or clarity; it invites accumulation. Suddenly you have more miscellaneous possessions because you have a drawer specifically for them. Using miscellaneous as a category promotes the retention of items that aren't important or useful, because it is a pseudo-organizing system.

If you take time to dismantle miscellaneous, you'll likely get rid of additional items, put a few with other like items, and possibly create a new, smaller category as well.

If you had junk drawers in your former homes or don't regularly re-evaluate the organization of your home, it will be easy to continue this bad habit. Defaults are devoid of thought and absent any intentional act of organizing.

Occasional labeling

If items are visible, often used, or stored in clear containers, labels aren't necessarily needed. When everything has a logical home, you'll intuitively know where to put things back.

For all other circumstances, it's worth adding a label, and more descriptive ones when items are in storage of any kind. Don't assume that you will remember things or think, *I'll label this later.*

Beyond labels, creating inventory lists for hard-to-reach areas or storage of any kind is a worthwhile strategy.

Aesthetic organizing

Design and aesthetics have a varying degree of importance to different people. If you've completed all of your work with alignment and intention up to this point, it's not "anti-minimalist" to purchase aesthetically pleasing organizing containers and other solutions to make your home feel the way you want it to.

While I urge you not to sacrifice function for form, focusing on the design of your space when organizing is the fun part. It may help you feel greater ownership of your space, solidify your organizing strategy and systems, and even make it more joyful to retrieve and put away items.

Deciding what to keep with clear intentions will accomplish a lot of the organizing work implicitly. Often, as you organize, you'll get rid of more things and see more opportunities to rearrange what's left. While there are many other organizing tactics and strategies, these will get you started in the direction of a minimalist lifestyle.

Put Lifestyle Changes into Practice

Now it's time to address the "non-stuff" stuff that makes up a significant portion of your lifestyle. Since you're developing a new, minimalist lifestyle, not just letting go of objects, the paring-down process must address things that take up our time and emotional bandwidth—not just our space. Putting aside what you do for a living and sleep, our remaining time is split into three general buckets: relationships, extracurriculars, and life administration. All three of these have a "stuff" component, but we also want to address the daily bandwidth they require and whether they belong in our lives based on how they align with our *whys*, values, goals, and priorities. We'll go through each bucket and address how to right-size them for our lives with a minimalist mindset.

Relationships

Relationships must be addressed in the same way as objects: what to let go of, what to reposition or use in a different way, and what you're missing that you need to seek out. They also connect to objects in ways that require unpacking aspects of the relationship in order to address the objects.

We engage in relationships at all levels: family, friends, acquaintances, professional peers, and the guy we trust at the auto repair shop. Relationships have histories, misunderstandings, ebbs and flows, and sometimes even a transactional nature. It's a broad bucket.

Relationships require developing, nurturing, redefining, and sometimes letting go. But often, we engage in relationships without enough intention about what we want, how they align with our values and priorities, and how we want to integrate them into our lives.

Because relationships are likely to have a strong emotional element, we shy away from getting deeply honest with ourselves about what different people mean to us and how we want this collage of people to fit into our overall lifestyle.

This resistance to addressing relationships also stems from the difficulty we all have with communicating emotions, concerns, and tricky truths. Or even the basics of communicating—for example, something as simple as "less texting and more phone calls."

Humans are social creatures. We need other people. We're faced with an epidemic of loneliness, distance between our loved ones, difficulties creating community, and a dearth of meaningful connections. And yet the truth is, when trying to establish more life alignment between goals, values, and what we actually enjoy, letting go of a friend whose values don't align with yours is part of creating a minimalist lifestyle.

Issues related to relationships always come up when I work with clients. The easiest issue to identify is memorabilia, the physical object component. Maybe some people are no longer in your life, but their stuff or the stuff they gave you still is (sometimes because of guilt). But paring down those possessions brings up issues associated with the relationships, which means it's more about the relationship than the object itself. So addressing non-tangible relationship questions is part and parcel of the paring-down process.

We also have relationships with people who are no longer living. These are still relationships and should be considered in this bucket. You may need to wrestle with the emotional weight of a parent who's passed away and how your relationship with them has played into how much of their stuff you've kept.

As you go through this paring-down process and move toward establishing your new lifestyle, be sure to identify how you want to incorporate all your relationships via the four actions (develop, nurture, redefine, let go). Make the connection between these relationship decisions and any impact they have on your physical space or lifestyle. Ensure your decisions are aligned with your values, goals, and priorities.

Extracurriculars

We're in a time of abundance: countless blogs and articles to read, shows to watch, online courses to take, hobbies to practice, volunteer work to do, exercise classes to try, and wood to whittle. We suffer from too many interests as much as we do from too much stuff. I'm defining an extracurricular as anything outside of work, relationship time, and life administration. Time and again, my clients have so many wonderful things they want to do that they feel stress around all this goodness.

With clarity on your priorities and a focus on streamlining your life in every possible way, you may find that you still have one too many interests to fit into your week. First, appreciate having the "problem" of abundance. Then get ready to make some tough decisions.

With my client Amir, single and in his thirties, with ample free time and many interests, we found a quarterly system to be the best approach. He listed his current interests: learning to bake bread, volunteering at the local bike repair shop, finishing coursework in mathematical concepts, and learning square dancing, just to start. There were some other hobbies, like learning to play the guitar, that were of interest to him but not nearly as much as these others. We chose one hobby for each quarter of the year so that, instead of spreading his time among all of them regularly, he could put more focused effort into a given target. If he wanted to re-up the next quarter, he could push the next interest down the line.

This approach led Amir to greater fulfillment of truly engaging with the interest, lack of "abundance stress," and a lot more clarity about what to do with his extra time. It also highlighted where he squandered some of his free time (endless perusal of dating apps) and what activities he needed to allot time for, like reading. Also, nixing the guitar from the list led him to pass along the used guitar that had been handed down to him to someone who really wanted it, ensuring it no longer took up any more physical or mental space. If he had decided not to learn guitar this year but planned to prioritize it next year, I would have advised him to keep the guitar, but put it away since it wasn't actively being used. And if he didn't prioritize it the following year, he would be ready to let it go.

Even when it doesn't make it to our list of goals and priorities, downtime is a necessity. We may be more active or more passive during this time, but we always want to be more intentional. An extracurricular for you might be as simple as time each week to sit in a chair and stare out the window. This counts as much as a personal hobby or a two-week vacation.

More general than extracurriculars alone, the idea of spending time and money on experiences rather than stuff is a compelling approach. However, it requires some caveats.

It's not minimalism if you run yourself into debt through experiences, especially if you are using those experiences as commodities—ways of making yourself look a certain way to others or to fill something that can only be filled by healing yourself. Shiny object syndrome exists with experiences too.

Ask yourself whether you really *enjoy* these experiences or you just *think* you'll enjoy them. Or do you think it's cool to like them—do you think they make you more impressive? Do you want them just for the story? Do you collect them like people collect books on their shelves? Are they an avenue for avoidance?

When paring down extracurriculars, you first need to create your list of interests, including what digital activities you're engaging in on your phone or computer. Include naps and any other interstitial activities. Within the downtime activities, you'll need to prioritize and likely cut some out. Be sure to evaluate whether you can let go of any physical objects related to the activities you've cut.

Some of your extracurricular activities may overlap with relationships. If you've developed relationships with the pickleball league you joined, you've reached a lovely minimalist efficiency of using your time to enhance these two buckets of your life. (On the other hand, if you hate playing pickleball but only do it because your friends like it, then you have some thinking to do about this particular extracurricular.)

Logistically, how do you fit in time for relationships and extracurriculars? That's life administration, which includes the way you calendar your life and how you remind yourself to "Call Mom."

Life Administration

What is life administration?
Life administration is the term I use to generally describe the tasks that help us be functioning members of society. Life administration spans from the must-dos like paying your taxes, doing the laundry, and renewing your car's registration, to truly optional tasks like renewing a magazine subscription. Some life administration tasks

are more day-to-day like sorting through the mail, while others are occasional like picking up your new pair of glasses.

Some life administration tasks are like getting gas: The impetus to do it is obvious and the consequences if you don't are clear. Others, like researching a better cellphone plan, are optional and less definitive in their parameters (e.g., how much time is spent on it versus how much money could be saved, and how to go about conducting this research).

All life administration tasks include the item that needs to be accomplished (e.g., landscaper's invoice paid, dry cleaning picked up) and the tactic to achieve it (e.g., send an email, errand). Without a system for organizing these tasks, they can get overwhelming and easily fall through the cracks. Fortunately, as part of your minimalist lifestyle, you can develop strategies to accomplish these tasks efficiently (e.g., pay the landscaper's invoice while checking email or set a timer to pay all the bills due for the month).

Common elements of life administration

The following are common formats for managing our life administration. Understanding them and then focusing on how to streamline the way you use them will help you make decisions about how to downsize and organize their digital and analog components.

Information. This includes paper documents and digital files. We also often store information in our email but don't classify it that way. Taking stock of where we store information and how we want to access it is key. Much like with our stuff, we panic over *what-ifs,* worrying that we'll need a specific piece of information one day, when often this never comes to pass or the consequences are far from dire. Information also suffers from the low-impetus-for-retrieval problem, so we tend to forget what information we have, even if it's well organized.

Communication. Consider how you'd like to conduct personal and life administration communications. Be honest with yourself about which communications are best suited for text, phone calls, emails, and in-person.

Task and project lists. Be careful not to confuse projects with tasks and remember that some tasks may have important subtasks. You need a single location to maintain an active task list. These represent the objectives you want to achieve over the course of a week or so. You can use this to create a daily to-do list to stay focused. Additionally, you can keep any number of project and idea lists, as long as they're stored in a place you can easily recall (i.e., there's an impetus for retrieval).

Calendar. Calendars are for events that occur at a specific time. In addition, a task that needs to occur during a specific time or that involves a large chunk of uninterrupted time (e.g., a call to your insurance company) may be best scheduled on your calendar, as well. Do you use a shared calendar? Or do you have multiple calendars that need to be synced (including an analog one)? Keep these potential complications in mind.

How to streamline life administration
Since life administration relates to some physical items, streamlining it requires making decisions about what life administration

elements you want to pare down and how to organize the tools (and systems) that support it.

Consider what life administration items (notebooks, calendars, and paperwork, for starters) can be pared down based on what tools you use and find most effective. During the organizing stage, develop a basic setup, like how to access sensitive documents and current projects files so you can easily address immediate needs.

Then, look at the tasks themselves—are they all necessary? Are they all valuable? Like everything else related to minimalism, life administration must fit into your vision and not conflict with your priorities. If you think they're must-dos, double-check that these connect tasks to your goals. Identify whether this task will help you achieve your goals and priorities (directly or indirectly), and at minimum, that it doesn't conflict with your values.

Aside from seeing where you can delete tasks that either aren't necessary or aren't enough of a priority, a minimalist framework will help you streamline the strategies and processes you use to complete them.

To downsize life administration tasks, identify your common task types, then categorize them into more general categories if that helps. You won't be able to do this in one sitting. Start the list now and keep it accessible so that, when you see yourself doing a life administration task you forgot about, you'll identify it as such and have a place to add it.

As you start analyzing your tasks, note what you struggle with: maybe it's running certain types of errands or anything related to finances. If so, consider hiring an accountant to save time and reduce stress and stop owning dry-clean-only clothing because upkeep is too time-consuming and pricey. Note whether the problem lies in the task, the format, or the tactic.

As you analyze, question all assumptions about whether specific tasks are important or necessary—or if you can address them in a more streamlined way with your newly developed minimalist mindset. It's easy to get caught in other bureaucracies and, with their influence, create our own. We never want to do more work than we have to.

Then, make some cuts or identify where a more streamlined approach can be taken. For example, you may decide to donate all those dry-clean-only clothes (cut), or you may decide to always call customer service instead of email because you find that way to be more efficient (streamline).

Another example is bill payment. You can't stop paying your bills, but you can rethink your approach. If you pay bills by mail, you may switch to autopay to save time and ensure you don't miss any payments. This may involve registering for online bill payment and shredding all past bills.

After determining what remains in your life administration bucket, you can organize it physically and digitally and determine how you want to handle the process of getting these tasks done. Consider devising rulesets (like we did with our stuff) and organizational systems, because we not only want to minimize time and effort spent on administration but we also want to avoid costly problems that we incur if we miss any tasks (e.g., forget to pay a parking ticket).

Things inevitably go wrong. There will be unavoidable hiccups (e.g., a computer crash) and unexpected events (e.g., medical issues). A credit card may get stolen, or you may have to find a new dentist. The more you have in order, the easier it will be to address these problems and ensure they are anomalies, not norms.

Often, digitizing seems to be the answer to everything. But the digital world can become a crutch since it doesn't "take up space." Do you keep every digital document file you ever created because it is mostly "unseen"? Probably ... until they take up too much space and you're in a panic with a hard drive at capacity, and you can never find what you're looking for anyway. As with all the stuff you accumulate in your home, the "piles" in the digital space can get too tall and unstable too. They're just much easier to ignore.

Just like there are bins you can organize your stuff in, the digital world offers a plethora of tools. Start with the most basic tool and then notice any pinch points or places where things fall through. List these. Then seek a tool that addresses your concerns. Don't "over-app," and try not to overlap apps.

Of course, your digital organizational tool collection has to be balanced by avoiding over-engineering and being okay with occasionally not having a document that you need. There is usually a way to handle these situations. Between the trade-off of occasionally not having something you need versus the cumbersome over-engineering as an alternative, the former always wins out.

It's easy to forget about relationships, extracurriculars, and life administration as part of the minimalism process because we tend to only think of downsizing and organizing as physical processes. Starting from the perspective of these buckets, rather than randomly sorting through any physical objects they relate to, will help you make clear and cohesive decisions in the appropriate context.

Good News and Bad News

Once you've created a vision and plan, and have pared down, organized, and implemented lifestyle changes, you'll probably wonder, "What now?" Here's the good news I haven't told you yet: As you go through your stuff, it's okay to identify things you need to acquire. In fact, I encourage it. Those things can be added as a list in your project plan. You may even choose to track the money you made from selling some items, any undeposited checks found, or canceled subscriptions or canceled storage unit fees to see how much you've saved and earned.

Only buy things now if they are replacements or necessities after completing most of your organizing or are organizing tools you're sure you need. Then, write a separate list for additional items to purchase. Prioritize the items on that list and determine the time frame for purchasing each. We'll review purchasing strategies in Part 7: Continuous Care.

But here's what I hope you don't see as bad news: You're not done. Iterating upon and maintaining your systems is the ongoing task of minimalism. That's why we call it a lifestyle and a practice. It can't be completed. It's most helpful to consider how you're going to care for your improved life while you're creating it.

Part VII

Continuous Care

Once your minimalism-related work has been primarily implemented, it's just the beginning of continuous care. This is the part that everyone forgets about or avoids. It doesn't come from a burst of energy or the need for a material catharsis. It doesn't have the exhilaration of countless bags hauled out of your home.

There is a danger in ignoring it. All your hard work and time will not see its potential. That's why we focused on mindset change and goal alignment so that it would not only be easier to let things go, but it'd also be easier to maintain the new life you created. It's most helpful to think about how you will maintain your improved home and lifestyle from the beginning and put prevention strategies into place to ensure you don't slip into old habits and find yourself in the same troubling place that brought you to this book.

But we first need to address the initial moments when you're faced with the space you've opened up in your home and schedule and prepare yourself for how to handle it.

How to Handle Emptiness

How do you feel about the growing emptiness— both physical and mental? The fear that without all the chaos you've created, you have, in fact, been hiding from something: a confrontation with the past, loneliness, uncertainty about the future, or feelings of failure found along the way.

While it may not be the driving force behind excess and disorganization, we want to keep that void far away. It's much like how sitting silently in meditation can be unnerving and uncomfortable.

What about the emptiness of not knowing yourself as well as you thought? While the practice of minimalism highlights and centers what's most meaningful, stripping away what's not can be surprisingly scary. Now with more time and space, you may realize you don't have as many meaningful relationships, interests, or goals in your life as you assumed. Emptiness helps us continue to discover meaning and rediscover what we want at this point in our lives. It's an opportunity.

Much like our desire to keep busy, to always want to feel desired and valued, we look for things outside of ourselves to keep us away from this empty space. Without the distraction of stuff out of place and piled high, consider: What drives you? Where do you fit in the world? What pulls at you now? What keeps you going?

We resist these uncomfortable questions, which is why we tend to choose a "something" over a "nothing." As you continue through this practice, pay attention to these fears so you have an opportunity to overcome them.

Aside from these more existential moments, the physical nature of emptiness causes us to want to fill the space. In the past, if a space was considered too empty, we'd feel the need to fill it rather than enjoy its openness or consider our home to be bigger than needed. That's the word we use: empty. Not full of potential memories or places to expand ourselves. We treat it like a problem that can only be solved with more stuff.

Why do we feel the urge to fill space? We've all been in social situations where we're suddenly struck by an awkward moment of silence. It feels like something has gone wrong or we've mistakenly turned into a dead end. Then, we look for an action as a solution, forgetting that doing nothing is also an action. So we begin to tell a story, ask a question, or talk about nothing. We try to fill the space because empty space can feel uncomfortable. The way we fill the space when we're in this mindset tends not to be meaningful or purposeful, but we do it anyway.

Many of us have had the beautiful experience of sitting in comfortable silence. We describe it this way because most silences are uncomfortable. We tend to define our relationships by how comfortable our silences are with the other person. When we don't desire to fill space, we can just be. Your home can be this way too.

Use your newfound space to widen your stance and stretch out your arms rather than seeking to box yourself. Space is what allows us to pause. Space is where we can find contentment, where we can reflect, and where we can just be. Space is a little bit of freedom.

Continuous care requires us to listen during the silence and not run back to former comforts. It requires us to hear our true selves and not overreact with old habits. Return to your *why*; ground yourself in your goals, priorities, and values. Investigate where the discomfort lives: Is it shame? Is it feelings of failure? Is it loneliness? Exercise your skills of observation and curiosity as you experience the empty wall or the blank day on your calendar. Resist impatience and going back to old distraction habits. Instead, explore why the discomfort is there and how you feel about it so you can make conscious, well-informed decisions.

Prevention and Maintenance
Are Crucial

The ongoing practice of minimalism is an act of continuous care. It's an opportunity to protect and cherish what you've created for yourself. It also gives you the opportunity to keep improving upon it. It's composed of two primary components: prevention and maintenance.

Prevention is an investment in keeping things simple and ensuring you don't have to go through another significant downsizing in the future. It involves making personal policy decisions about what you'll let into your home before you are confronted with a decision in the moment. While the focus has been on letting go, that effort will be a temporary gesture if you don't stop more stuff from coming in. Learning to let go is different than learning to keep out. Though with your organized, trimmed-down home and clarity on your life priorities, it should be less difficult, and you will be more inspired and determined to work through obstacles.

Remember that material things used to tempt you for a reason. A minimalist mindset doesn't completely inoculate you from consumerism or sporadic desires. There may be moments, at least at first, when saying no to things freely offered feels uncomfortable. This takes some getting used to. This is why the reasons behind this mindset shift are paramount to success. You have to see stuff differently and connect the dots between stuff, stress, and wastefulness. That's why we go deep. Refer to Part 3: Question Everything and Part 4: Rebuild Your Mindset to review the mindset changes that will boost your prevention skills.

The better you are at prevention, the easier maintenance will be. Maintenance involves obvious things like staying on top of product returns, bill payments, repairing things, monitoring your task list and calendar, and keeping your home tidy and organized. Efficient and effective maintenance involves determining whether the systems you put into place work. If you still have trouble finding things or putting them away, is there a better solution you can try? Maintenance is best served by a schedule and developing supportive routines.

Once you're in maintenance mode, you can conduct some of the more minor organizing projects that weren't necessary during your initial work. As we discussed, it's not worth over-organizing when there are diminishing returns or when organizing too much can make something more challenging to maintain. Maintenance work can include some of the more detailed projects you set aside like going through that box of kids' artwork you collected to create a scrapbook of their work. Or skim through the organized shelf of old journals at your leisure, ultimately letting them go.

Experiencing your new minimalist lifestyle will build your self-confidence and competence and, at minimum, show you that even a 5 percent improvement in your lifestyle is worthwhile. These wins will create a positive feedback loop to continue caring for your simplified life. You may even look forward to moments when you can re-evaluate and revise aspects of your home and lifestyle. Find the joy in continuous care to create the energy and impetus you had when initially embarking on your minimalist practice.

How to Practice Prevention

The less you bring into your home, the less you have to maintain and potentially pare down later. It's simple, but consumption creep happens when we're not looking because we're inundated with advertisements and social pressures. We can easily let our guard down and fall back into bad habits. So you need a plan.

To bring in less, you'll rely on the mindset change and honesty you've been developing and put purchasing prevention strategies in place. To exercise discernment, apply what you learned in Part 3: Question Everything and Part 4: Rebuild Your Mindset: engaging in delayed gratification, saying no to the status quo, identifying the hidden costs of stuff, and not succumbing to the fleeting glee trap. Just as you may have employed numerous *what-ifs* and rationalizations when deciding whether to keep your possessions, you may have let these thoughts lead you to buy things you didn't need. That's another bad habit to break.

There is another layer of prevention: preventing yourself from being tempted in the first place. Some strategies to reduce temptation include unsubscribing to catalogs and store newsletters (not worth the coupons they send to stay subscribed) and no longer using online "window shopping" as a way to cure boredom. Avoid putting yourself in tempting situations so that you don't have to expend energy to resist purchasing or find yourself in endless internal negotiations.

Part of prevention is also choosing better products when you need to acquire something. You'll become a more responsible purchaser by considering how a particular product aligns with your goals and lifestyle, evaluating the quality of products for longevity and durability, and ensuring that these products align with your *why*. This way, "curating your toolbox" happens when both paring down and purchasing.

Now let's take a look at a handful of prevention strategies to sharpen your skills.

Calm the pulse of impulse buying

Impulse buying is just that: an impulse. It's difficult to apply logical thinking to purchase decisions when we go straight from seeing something we (think we) want to purchase to making the purchase in almost an instant. That's a reaction, not a choice.

Impulse buys of the past were a reflection of not having clarity about what you own, where it lives in your home, and your purchasing priorities. Even with mindset change, impulse purchasing can still happen. The good news is that you can expect this problem to come up less. But you still need to prepare.

We have to learn how to interrupt the impulse and all the ways we try to rationalize once it happens. Meaning, it might not be the initial impulse that hooks you, but after you first say no to the initial impulse, you succumb to, "But on the other hand ..." That's where the rationalizing begins. For example:

"But I've worked hard, so I deserve this!" (You may have worked hard, but that doesn't qualify you for a brand-new car.)

"But the newest smartphone has all of these new cool features." (Are these features things you've needed, or do you just think you need them now that you've learned about them? What about your working phone with features you don't use?)

"It's such a great price. I can't miss a deal like this!" (Deals are figments of our imaginations; sales are relative. Eighty percent off something you don't need is still 20 percent more than you need to spend.)

"I love the new colors and styles of the season. I want what's in fashion now." (Timeless pieces will keep your closet manageable. Are any of these styles something you'll wear when they're no longer a trend?)

Remember how draining internal negotiations can be and how much they contribute to your ongoing decision fatigue. You might get some use out of your purchase, but is it worth the time, money, and internal debate?

Reducing exposure and temptation, as discussed previously, is particularly helpful when combating impulse purchases. But you can take it further by removing your saved credit cards from online shopping sites, only allowing purchases one day a week, or requiring yourself to leave something in an online cart for a certain amount of time before making a final decision.

Test out different strategies and see which ones work best for you.

Avoid purchases for future potential projects

Starting projects or simply buying the materials needed to start a project before we are quite ready to begin sets us up for failure. It highlights that we want to do the easy parts of those projects as we daydream about the finished product. We love crossing "purchase" off a list, but we are usually less willing to commit to the project itself.

Maybe you think that buying something for a project will "hold you accountable." This is the same idea behind the gym membership. Yes, sometimes you'll push yourself to go to the gym because you know you're paying for it. Sometimes that helps motivate us, but it doesn't mean our workout efforts will be genuine. Will you do a great job working out, making each minute count? Will it help you address any of the underlying issues that hold you back from working out in the first place? No, it's just a little game that can sometimes give you a boost. Be careful when you use accountability as your reasoning. Sometimes it's only a well-dressed excuse.

Sometimes you can dip into a project before really starting. Maybe you've always wanted to knit. Instead of buying all the yarn, needles, and books to get started, ask someone you know whether you can borrow a pair of needles and if they can teach you how to do the most basic stitch. More on this when we discuss the "stuff test-drive" in the next section.

Now let's say you believe you're really committed to starting a scrapbooking project. First, think specifically about what you want to scrapbook. Collect all the photos you'll use. Based on that, start thinking about what design style you'd like to employ. Consider whether you need one or multiple scrapbooks, depending on the theme and number of pictures. Decide when you'll work on this project, perhaps carving time on your calendar. Then, after determining your budget, buy the materials to start the project. With your new materials in hand, bring together all your supplies on the day you begin scrapbooking. At this point, you've invested more into the project and have a basic plan. That vision can morph as you engage in the project, but you aren't getting distracted by the fun and ease of making a purchase in lieu of completing the project itself.

If you are thinking, *Well, I don't have time to do all of those steps*, or *I have to take advantage of just the few moments I have when I have them*, you don't have time for scrapbooking. Avoid making your life more difficult by wasting time and money on supplies and mental energy thinking about scrapbooking and how you never seem to get to it, all resulting in you feeling bad about yourself. Remember those piles of shame we talked about earlier?

Prevent never-to-be-started projects from entering your home from the start.

Conduct a "stuff test-drive"

It's fun to show up at a car dealership and take a test-drive. While this is an obvious ploy to get you to fall in love with the car and purchase it on the spot, there's a practical side to it. You're about to make a really big purchase, and no matter what you've read about the car, you won't know whether it's right for you until you see how the seat feels, how the car brakes, the car's turning radius, and generally how it feels to drive. While most of our other purchases aren't nearly this expensive, we can take a lesson from this approach.

One way to test-drive an item is to borrow it. Borrowing can help us reduce unfettered excitement and lessen the impulse to purchase. Granted, you need to know someone who has the product you have your eye on and is willing to let you try it out. If you can't take it home with you, have an in-depth conversation about it and conduct a test-drive at their place.

The idea of borrowing in our communities is starting to become more accessible. Often we think of borrowing as something we can only do with books, and only at a library. But libraries across the US are utilizing their borrowing infrastructure to lend out non-media items such as tools. And some community groups host libraries for items like dishes or décor. Apps and websites have been developed to coordinate similar sharing efforts. Many of these options aim to replace the need to buy new items at all, which is optimal, but they can offer opportunities for accessible test-drives.

Another test-drive strategy is to buy a less expensive, used, or trimmed-down version of the item you want. You may discover that top-tier products have far more bits of functionality than are necessary for your needs. Often you don't need all the bells and whistles you'd be paying extra for. Still, you can sell or give away the first model you tried if you want to upgrade. Or you might find that what you have suffices and keep it instead. Warning: This strategy can backfire if you end up keeping the less expensive version but then think, *Why not have two?* So in addition to what you already have, you purchase the new, upgraded version.

Another option is to use a placeholder for the item—something you already have that can give you a sense of whether you need to make a purchase. For example, if considering buying an e-reader, you might try reading an e-book on your phone to see if you like reading books digitally. Or if you want a riser for your laptop, try a pile of books first. This strategy is helpful when organizing too. I encourage clients to use boxes or bins they already own to makeshift their new organizing systems. After it's clear what possessions they'll keep, and where they'll keep them, they can purchase organizing products that will suit their specific needs and aesthetics.

The stuff test-drive can be completed using an array of different tactics: borrowing, renting, buying a cheaper pared-down version, or using a placeholder item. The end goal is to minimize purchases and, when purchasing, have a better sense of exactly what you want. Drive before you buy.

Start a purchasing journal

If you've been on a diet or nutrition plan, you may be familiar with a food diary, in which you chronicle each morsel of food you eat each day. The benefit is that we're mindful about each bite because we have to write it down. Also, our memories are rarely accurate, so what we think we've eaten in a day or week is often not the same as what has actually occurred. Our minds create a narrative that doesn't consistently have accurate data to support it. This aligns with the adage, "You can't manage what you don't measure."

The same concept can be applied with purchasing. Whatever you think you buy or how much you spend on different types of things is probably not an accurate representation of what you actually purchase. Knowing exactly what you buy, why you buy it, and how much you spend is a targeted way to undo bad habits and make more-aware choices.

My client Faith uses a basic spending tracker app. She inputs everything she buys, down to gum at a convenience store or ten bucks she owes a friend. She says this has helped her fully acknowledge each purchase's spend and monetary value. It's helped her tremendously in getting out of debt and making her feel greater agency. Spending didn't just "happen." She was able to take greater responsibility.

While I'm not encouraging you to be as thorough as Faith, you can identify types of purchases to track. These might be any discretionary spends like coffee or a manicure. As we discussed in the hidden costs of stuff, aggregate sites like Amazon and other larger stores don't make our categories of spending clear on our credit statements. You can use your purchase journal to track these purchases specifically so you have a full picture of your categories of spending when you review your finances each month. Or you can keep a purchasing journal for only a week or month to learn more about your habits.

Sustainability-driven prevention

As we touched on in the I Care About the Environment chapter, waste happens every time a product is created—waste we don't see. Part of prevention is preventing toxic, wasteful, and/or new (when it can be reused) items from entering your home. Another part is making better purchases when you really do need something. Cheap products may save us money in the short term but will cost more in the long run. If it's a discretionary purchase and you can't afford to buy a durable, non-toxic version, it's often better not to buy it at all instead of buying a cheap alternative. Then you can budget to buy the higher-quality version when you can afford it.

Aside from reducing what you acquire, try to reuse and repurpose as much as you can within your home as part of maintenance. When purchasing, prioritize reuse by shopping at thrift stores, reuse boutique stores, vintage stores, and consignment shops. High-end purveyors of previously worn clothing curate more attractive collections, selling lightly used clothing and accessories. There are plenty of apps that allow you to shop reused goods from home. However, you still have to exercise awareness by only acquiring what you need, even though previously used items are typically less expensive.

Aside from buying used and more durable items, consider buying items that you'll be able to reuse, especially when it means avoiding single-use, disposable items. For example, reusable silicone bags for leftovers (and pretty much anything else you'd put in a single-use sandwich bag) are a great example of a "zero-waste" purchase.

Zero waste aims to avoid as much waste as possible by reducing, reusing, recycling, and composting in lieu of sending things to the landfill. Much like a minimalist lifestyle, you move toward zero waste as a practice rather than a realistic destination. Zero waste strategies can be incorporated into your purchasing and prevention system. For more information on zero waste, check out Bea Johnson's book, *Zero Waste Home: The Ultimate Guide to Simplifying Your Life by Reducing Your Waste*.

This focus on prevention may start to feel rigid, like you're taking the little things too seriously. If you get to that point, loosen the reins a bit. We all impulse-buy sometimes. We just want these to be exceptions and not the rule. And then as the exceptions, they'll feel better as a fun indulgence that you'll appreciate more.

Make It Easy

After putting minimalism into practice, maintenance helps us keep what we organized *organized*, manage new objects that enter our homes, and implement systems to keep our lives running smoothly. While we looked at streamlining life administration in the Put Lifestyle Changes into Practice chapter, most of the work you'll do occurs as part of maintenance.

Through an emphasis on maintenance, you improve and adapt as necessary. This highlights the iterative nature of a minimalism practice and speaks to why continuous care is so important—all this work is limited in benefit if it doesn't stick. Helpful components of maintenance include creating a maintenance schedule and establishing routines, habits, and rituals.

Maintenance schedule

Effective maintenance is a simple schedule that is tracked and adhered to. It keeps life running smoothly and minimizes the drama of unexpected problems occurring. Without (mostly) scheduled maintenance, it's easy to drop the ball on certain tasks.

Develop a schedule based on what is reasonable for you. This schedule is central to your work; do not treat it as an afterthought.

The schedule should include not only the concrete actions you plan to take but also reminders that uphold the decisions you've made to maintain this lifestyle. I prefer schedules that don't involve many constant activities. They quickly become annoying. If the schedule does not include regular tasks, though, you'll forget you even have a schedule. And miss some basic upkeep. Here are a few ideas to get you started that can be adapted to your own needs, priorities, and proclivities.

Daily. Put away items missing from their homes, including kitchen items on the counter and in the sink. Put clothes away. If you do it daily, it's an easy add-on as you move through your space. Make your bed as a morning meditation of humble gratitude. Not keeping a lot on your bed makes this easier.

Weekly. Plan your week. Do laundry. Go grocery shopping. Clean a couple of things you don't clean more regularly but feel a month would be too long to wait on (like a bathroom).

Monthly. Create a financial day once a month to ensure all bills are paid, spending is reviewed, all accounts are double-checked, and during which you can handle anything else out of routine that has come up. Having significantly less stuff but still forgetting to deposit the check your Great-Aunt Martha gave to you, missing bill payments, or scrambling at the last minute to submit your tax return completely misses the lifestyle part of life administration. This tactic builds financial confidence and prevents things from slipping through the cracks.

Quarterly. For things that don't need attention monthly, this is a nice place to stash seasonal things. Your quarters may not line up perfectly every three months; favor what is logical for your needs rather than trying to fit a specific date. This is also a great increment for life planning and a review of priorities and goals.

Yearly. Schedule one yearly financial review and planning day. Make your annual medical appointments. Conduct once-a-year cleaning projects. Homeowners in particular can use this review to ensure home maintenance isn't neglected. It's also an opportunity for "minimalism maintenance" activities such as going through your home to donate or otherwise get rid of items you no longer need.

Aside from creating a clear, iterated, specific, and responsibility-inducing schedule, you need to integrate it in a way in which it can't be forgotten about. For non-daily items, you can add dates to your calendar in advance. You can print the schedule as a document you post to your refrigerator, the inner liner of your planner, your entry door, in your office … wherever you're most likely to see it. For items you're concerned about forgetting or ignoring, consider using the reminder function on your computer or phone.

Your schedule will be even more effective if you include goal reminders. These will remind you of the importance of these efforts, mapping them back to their intended purpose while also giving you a reason to update your schedule if your goals have changed.

Accountability is key. Share with a bossy friend who would love nothing more than to tell you what to do and hold you accountable. There are accountability apps or apps that apply the reverse of positive reinforcement.

Routines, habits, and rituals

Minimalism provides maximum room for spontaneity. Because there's simply more room in your life. Enjoy it! But that room is in part created by having routines in place like the maintenance schedule described above. Routines, habits, and rituals make us more resilient when unexpected things come up and keep us clearheaded about what we want to do.

Routines are specific behaviors frequently repeated, like brushing your teeth in the morning. Some routines are habits, meaning you have the impulse to complete that routine with little or no thought. Brushing your teeth may be a habit, while taking a jog in the morning may be a routine because you do it every weekday morning, but each time, it's a struggle to motivate yourself.

Design and iterate your routines and habits around the important elements of your minimalist lifestyle. If one of your top three priorities currently is to get in shape, developing a schedule for your workouts and creating routines around them are essential.

While productivity experts and lifestyle designers will promote certain routines and habits, don't try to make them work for you if they don't. Return to the deep honesty with yourself and what works best for you. You get your best work done in the evening, not the morning? Great. Meditation not your jam? No problem.

The value of routines lies in their capacity to improve your chances of reaching your goals and in boosting your confidence and competence overall. Minimalism helps us identify areas in which building routines and habits are most worthwhile and in which minimalism makes the space we need to develop them.

A strategy to develop a habit is to pair an unwanted task with a desired reward. Align the times you work on items in your schedule with something special: reading for leisure, going to bed early, a careless hour of YouTube video watching, or other mindless internet procrastination. A cookie. You can also piggyback on a routine that's working if the activity is related.

Another way to build a habit may involve investing in a product you really like. For example, my client Esther has difficulty building habits but responds well to aesthetics. To bring a reusable bag with her when shopping instead of using disposable bags, she needed a bag that she really liked and found to be aesthetically pleasing. This is also an example of where strategic purchasing can lead to proper prevention (in this case, extraneous disposable bags). If you want to learn more about how to develop habits, consider reading *Atomic Habits* by James Clear.

Rituals are cousins to routines and habits and dovetail nicely in pursuing Meaningful Minimalism. Rituals are more purpose- and meaning-driven routines. It's an attitude difference; both are implemented with consistency and clarity. But rituals lend themselves to the more meaningful elements of life, while routines can cover some of the more challenging items you want to complete.

I consider making my bed each morning a ritual in which I feel humble and grateful for beginning a new day, whereas folding laundry and putting it away is a routine.

Developing your routines, habits, and rituals is a fundamental component of the continuous care process, ensuring you implement your vision easily, confidently, and with a greater sense of purpose.

Caring for your minimalist lifestyle through active and intentional maintenance provides you with the most room for the things you love and allows you to live an aligned life. From ensuring you replace the air filters in your home to washing the dishes, maintenance work is the unsung hero of our lives. Be sure to treat it with the same level of importance as letting go of physical objects in your home. As you earn back this time, grow a greater appreciation for it.

Keep Going

Exploring newly emptied spaces with curiosity, implementing prevention practices, and developing maintenance schedules and routines are all strategies that will make up your continuous care practices from the onset. But over time, these practices will need to evolve. The things you decide to let go of or reorganize when revisiting your stuff may change in nature. Your interests will evolve, as will your phase in life. Priorities shift, what gives us purpose shifts, our *whys* shift—all of which are changes that can cascade down to our possessions and how we live our lives in general. You may have to redefine what's most meaningful to you and readjust your home and lifestyle accordingly. Being aware of these changes while remaining committed to your minimalist lifestyle benefits from mindfulness, inspiration, and education.

A minimalist lifestyle doesn't inoculate you from distractions or unanticipated situations arising. Sometimes life is simply consuming, and we need to be aware enough not to let it overwhelm us. That's where mindfulness comes in. I've used the term *mindfulness* to convey a general idea: awareness in the present moment. Mindfulness is not a separate practice as much as it's a way of being, not too dissimilar from having a minimalist mindset. That's why mindfulness alongside minimalism is essential. They inform each other in downsizing, organizing, and continuing care processes. Mindfulness offers us an honest look at how we feel about the big stuff and where minor adjustments are needed. So be sure to develop mindfulness through whatever strategy works best for you, whether it be meditation, taking daily walks, breathwork, journaling, or training yourself to pause before reacting or making decisions.

As the exhilaration of cleared-out spaces and the rhythm of new routines wear off, you may need inspiration to keep up your continuous care efforts. Maybe it's reading something about minimalism every month. Maybe it's spending an analog day in silence and nature. Maybe it's looking at a photo that represents what you're doing this all for. Maybe, under the cover of night, it's looking at organizing porn. (You've done the behind-the-scenes work; you've earned this guilty pleasure!) Consider what inspiration will most support you and start integrating it now. Inspiration will help you continue this practice when it starts to feel challenging.

You've read this book because you wanted to learn. That education is not yet complete. Many skills and areas of knowledge can augment what you've learned and the work of minimalism. It might be to learn more about how to conduct home repairs, mend clothing, sustainability topics like zero waste, and personal finance. Think about where you felt ill-informed during the downsizing process or what maintenance work could be improved on or made more manageable with additional knowledge. Also, consider educating others about your experiences. You can become someone else's source of inspiration.

Keep going and growing.

The Real Self-Care

From the initial shock of empty spaces to preventing stuff and bad habits from creeping back in, minimalism is not a one-and-done effort to purge possessions from your home. These efforts should not be afterthoughts. Awareness, honesty, a focus on meaning, and mindset change are the skills you'll hone and employ to elevate your life with ease continuously. As you continue caring for your improved home and lifestyle, you'll truly care for yourself. That's been the point all along.

Now you can recalibrate, reset, and renew. You are more adaptable and living in alignment.

Conclusion: You're Ready

As you see, minimalism has very little to do with stuff. It's all about honesty, reclaiming your agency, and building a life around what's most meaningful to you.

See, it was you this whole time. You were looking externally for meaning, validation, and passing off your agency. You were looking to the past to navigate the future. You were just trying to feel safe and surround yourself with the things you thought would do that for you.

But you have control. You only need to be honest with yourself and others. Define and always stay connected to your *why*, North Star, priorities, and goals. Build the resilience to not be reactive to the current trends or news cycles. If you confront the more complex choices, your minimalist lifestyle will become the singular answer to many of your current stressors.

Meaningful Minimalism is a tool that I've described in detail, but it is beside the point. This is about taking your head out of the sand. Realizing that this work is the most important you'll do. Because it's the truth: the truth of who you are and who you want to be.

The truth always hurts, at least a little bit. Pain is caused by separation, and you are separating from your past self and past worldview, which included many ideas you once thought were true. Not to mention a sweater you used to wear all the time and a set of dishes you'll never use again.

Leading a simpler life in which you are more in touch with your reality rather than hiding behind the piles of stuff in your life allows space for your true dreams, not the things that have substituted for dreams.

Don't become a minimalist. Become the best version of yourself. Own your life, not your stuff.

And remember:

Minimalism is a process, a practice, and a lifestyle.

You are an evolving being.

Care for yourself.

Don't worry so much.

Afterword

You might be wondering what to do with this book (if you have a physical copy) now that you've read it. It's a test of the system. Here are a few considerations:

- Consider keeping it if you plan to use it as a reference guide.
- Do not put it in a storage unit or under your bed.
- Do not give it to someone who doesn't explicitly want it...but if you know someone who does, please pass it along!
- If you don't want to keep it and don't have someone to give it to, donate or sell it.

You can inspire others by discussing the book with them, creating a book club, or simply being the change you wish to see in the world.

Thank you for reading and taking the time to consider a new way of thinking and living.

Acknowledgments

The support and inspiration afforded to me in the process of writing this book reminds me that, like minimalism, writing a book is not entirely a solitary sport. From various writing groups in Austin, Texas, to random dinner party discussions, I appreciate each moment that contributed to this book's creation.

My clients, through the intimate views of their struggles, the depth and vulnerability of our conversations, and their trust in me to devise solutions to help them, contributed heavily to the book's content. In particular, I'd like to acknowledge my first client, Betsy Mendelsohn. Thanks for taking a chance on me and offering your support as I began my business.

To my parents, Sue and Bernie Zycherman: Mom, while this is a book about minimalism, you seemed interested from the beginning about what the book would say about you. I hope you're not disappointed! I hope both of you see how you were honored in this book. From providing endless content fodder to being champions of my business, even when I knew it caused you great anxiety for me to be out on my own, *thank you.*

To my brother, Marc Zycherman, and sister-in-law, Kristen Zycherman: So many of your insights, Kristen, are woven into this book. And Marc, you inspired so much of my work and how I work with clients who have similar challenges to you. I always wanted to build your confidence.

To my sister, Lisa Zycherman: Since you used to help edit my English papers, I couldn't have been more excited to get back your beta review comments. As always, they were insightful. And required me to do a lot more work. Your support of this book development, not to mention my business, is incalculable. I can only wish you were more disorganized so I could be of greater help to you.

To my other beta readers, Ari Frankel, Jocelyn Arem, and Emily Shaughnessy: You all volunteered for this work before I even asked. It wasn't easy to share such a rough draft with people I respect and admire, but you all gave helpful feedback and insights without knocking down my confidence. I'm so grateful. Jocelyn, as a beta reader and in your own pursuit of simplicity, you've always been so good at reflecting back what you've learned from me, how you've applied it to your life, and the result it's had—even when reading a messy, pre-copyedited draft of my book.

To Meghan Bogaerts: You gave me feedback on the original iteration of this book, which helped build my confidence that my ideas could really become a worthwhile book. You've been a trusted confidant, particularly in the writing arena.

To Erica Ross, my friend, the muse behind this book, the inventor of *minimalish,* and a stalwart champion of all my minimalism-driven work: Thank you for your support, inspiration, and belief that I'll become famous one day.

An extra thank you to my incredible partner, Sami Khalil: You told me that hearing I was a minimalist was one of the reasons you asked me out. Since then, you've lived with me through the intensity of bringing this project to life and supporting it every step of the way.

Aside from the volunteer support of my community and family, I hired some incredibly talented individuals to help shape this book into something readable.

To my developmental editor, Sarah Welch: My biggest fear was that your comments would be too light and positive. My other biggest fear was that I'd learn that my book was crap and in need of a complete overhaul. Fortunately, you found a balance and gave me clear direction on how to incorporate changes and finish my first book.

To my copyeditor, Andrea Vanryken: Thanks for the swift and thorough help, as well as your great ideas for renaming some chapters.

I couldn't have reached this personal and professional milestone without all of your unique support.

Bonus

Looking for help implementing what you've learned?

Get your free copy of this book's companion workbook to support your progress: www.meaningfulminimalism.com/bonus

Thank You for Reading!

Thank you for reading my book!

Please take two minutes to leave a helpful review on the website you purchased the book from or on Goodreads.

Thanks so much for your support!
Dara Zycherman

About the Author

Dara Zycherman is a minimalist lifestyle coach and founder of the company Less Equals More. She is a frequent speaker at organizations including TEDx, Capital One, and AMD, and her work has been featured in *Apartment Therapy* and *Minimalism Life*. She lives in Austin, Texas.

Cover design by Tim Barber, Dissect Designs
Photo by Samantha Robinson

www.ingramcontent.com/pod-product-compliance
Lightning Source LLC
Chambersburg PA
CBHW070907130626
46555CB00001B/35